THE BOOK OF FEAR

VOL. 1

BILLY PEDRO

Independent Publishing Network

The Book of Fear. Vol 1
ISBN: **978-1-83853-329-8**
eBook ISBN: **978-1-83853-253-6**
Printed in the United Kingdom

Publisher: Independent Publishing Network.
Publication date: June 2020
ISBN: **978-1-83853-329-8**
Author: Billy Pedro
Email: Info@billypedro.com
Website: Billypedro.com

Please direct all enquiries to the author.

The British Library has catalogued the original trade paperback edition.

The Book of Fear Volume 1 / Billy Pedro

Dedication

To all new born that will experience unidentified feelings in their environment and cultivate a character through their cognitive; hope this book influences the perception of things around you.

To every boy and girl experiencing fear at every stage of growth, hope your feelings are understood by the environment you live in through this book.

To every young adult in school, college, university or working, hope you thrive in your individual environment and you find this book useful in your personal development paths.

To every victim of circumstances of fear, hope you can find a way out through this book and realign your self-confidence through understanding of the issues surrounding you.

To every parent who is a champion doing the best they can to raise their family, hope you can find this book useful in understanding your strong influence on your family and your environment. Hope this book enhances your decision as you succeed.

To all business owners and business managers, hope this book helps in maximising productivity in your business.

To all leaders, hope this book can enhance your direction as you lead and operate with empathy for a better outcome.

To every race, culture, religion and nation in any form of uncertainty at this time, hope this book can help you retrace your steps to rediscover your potential values and direct you to your rightful path.

To everyone reading this book, this is dedicated to you. Hope this book liberates and helps in finding yourself. Hope it helps you reflect on good ethics of life and enhance your responses to challenges.

Contents

Preface

The word "fear" in itself can make us tremble in silence. As humans, in order for us to move forward from this silent reaction and other associated feelings, we must intentionally collate facts, history and narratives, so we are able to further analyse our perceptions. In turn, we can identify rational or irrational fear reactions, which have created solutions, corruption or, in some cases, destruction.

The Book of Fear explores the function of our fear, embellished with experience, to determine its purpose–or lack of it.

The Book of Fear considers our fear reactions in context; this is to explore the origin and state of mind that demonstrates fear in us, compared with the usual narrative of simply judging our reactions. It aims to explain and reflect on our reactions, which are birthed from situations of perceived fear, and, subsequently, to dissect the often unrecognised, counter-reactions to fear that make our situation affect our actions. From this, we are able explore the possible methods by which these reactions can be modified to better equip humanity.

The Book of Fear also looks deep into the stages of fear we experience – both before and after our reaction – to redefine and better our understanding of what fear really is, our perception of it and what use it could be for us as humans.

The Book of Fear explains our communication and interactions with each other regarding fear to better our understanding of individuals' experiences and behaviours, which are deemed to be either logical or illogical. During this process of gaining understanding, there is still a high level of respect for the background behavioural data collated, as well as empathy, and a consideration for the human ethics and principles that bring about change.

The Book of Fear delves into the differences between, mutual exclusivity of and psychology of phobias and fear, to understand our thought processes, our actions and reactions, the outcomes, and the psychological effects of both. By looking at our beliefs, ethics, lifestyle and other factors, we will be able to gain insight into how we can handle our feelings with respect to fear, individually and collectively.

The Book of Fear will be broken into a series of volumes to provide simultaneously both a broad and an explicit experience of possible situations, which will lead to developing a characterisation of our fear, to achieve additional and more beneficial outcomes, where needed.

Fear in Context

Creation

Defining Fear

Fear is relative, and the idea of fear is used and experienced in many ways to control, amend, manage, lead, manipulate, scaremonger, or just to keep people or an environment on its toes for a certain purpose. Although, sometimes, fear has no purpose.

Fear, in all contexts, can make us superhuman. We can take on anything when we are afraid. Our fear can push us to creating solutions to problems, building, destroying and creating possibilities when it is in full effect.

In light of this, we can conclude that fear could be a realm. A realm in the context of fear could mean a higher or a different plane of consciousness. Obviously, this couldn't be an actual place, but it is a psychological reaction that is triggered by the amygdala. The amygdala is a cluster of nuclei located in the temporal lobe of the brain, committed to detecting the emotional salience of stimulus. This means that the more significant the stimuli, the quicker the detection and the greater the reaction. Without delving too deeply into the details regarding human brain cells, the amygdala is said to be responsible for the perception of our emotions, as well as controlling our aggressive reaction. This requires closer scrutiny in order to gain insight as to whether the amygdala is just a receptor or a detector of the emotional salience of the stimuli, and also to determine the actual output of the reaction. One must happen before the other.

Cultivated Reaction

Our first reaction to any unidentified event is surprise

Fear and Reactions

Logically, the idea of "garbage in, garbage out" provides the best approach to understanding what the amygdala might do.

There is no smoke without fire. We must receive or perceive something before we respond. The process of perception only works when there is detection, which is the first action of the amygdala and the reaction is the second; everything else is felt afterwards. Anger is a processed reaction, but sadness is a fluid, reactive emotion that allows fear to determine what our processed reaction should be. Our first reaction to any unidentified event is surprise, and that surprise triggers fear. Fear then processes it to suggest some sort of reaction, which could be anger, happiness, comfort, sadness, joy, flight, fight or protection.

The amygdala also stores memories of events and the emotions attached to those memories, so that an individual may be able to recognise similar events in the future. The problem with these stored memories and the attached emotions are the cultivated reactive pattern of behaviour. These memories also affect our fixed reaction to similar events, where we may have stored a negative or even a positive reaction to a certain perception, but our reaction might need to be different for other similar events.

The Sound of Fear

A concluded reaction to sound

Pleasant and Unpleasant Sounds

Sound can be used as an example when explaining memories, attached emotion and reaction in an environment, in an effort to break down the receptive and reactive parts of our amygdala. A startling sound may be a surprise to us when we are not familiar with the perceived sound, and we may be totally unable to identify a sound when we are unsure where the sound is coming from. Once the sound has registered with us, we may relate to the sound as being very loud, a surprise or unidentified, but when we are able to change that memory to a more understandable one, our reaction may then alter, and the sound may become more of a stimulating type of sound. In this context, a stimulating type of sound is one that triggers a neutral reaction, or a raised level of physiological or nervous activity in our body.

A stimulating sound is the next level above a startling sound, where we become fully aware of the presence of the sound only for the purpose of stimulation, which doesn't create or require any other emotional reaction.

A pleasant sound is a reasoned reaction to an identified sound that gives us a relaxing, pleasing, sweet, satisfying, enjoyable, agreeable, likeable, nice or friendly feeling. This can also be assumed to be the next level after stimulation, where we have been able to place, build or cultivate some likeable emotion towards an identified sound.

An unpleasant sound –which is a discomforting, annoying, irritating, unlikeable, disruptive, disturbing, disagreeable, unattractive or unfriendly noise – also seems to generate a reasoned reaction. This can also be assumed to be the next level after stimulation, when we have been able to place, build or cultivate an unpleasant emotion with respect to an identified sound.

The sound in question may also be based on our perspective, and the memories cultivated in our reaction may change due to an altered environment or circumstances. We may tolerate certain sounds better on some occasions, for other reasons best known to ourselves.

Emotional Quotient (EQ) and Intelligence Quotient (IQ) of Fear

What makes us equal to animals

Our ability to manage what started out as fear to become a neutral, pleasant, unpleasant or circumstantial emotion requires an intelligence quotient (IQ) and emotional quotient (EQ).Our IQ is our ability to reason and solve problems at both acquired and required mental and physical levels of growth. Our EQ delves further into our adequacies in our self-awareness, empathy and sensitive management of our surroundings. We can develop our IQ, and we may develop EQ, but the amygdala is innate.

The amygdala is human. The amygdala is our learning faculty; it is our emotion. The amygdala is what makes us equal to animals, as they each have an amygdala too. As a matter of fact, animals' survival depends on it.

The EQ is what separates humans from animals. It has been proven that the sense of fear is lost when the amygdala is removed from an animal's brain, and that a similar result has been seen in humans. A person without an amygdala will approach danger like it's nothing, because they have no recognition that it is classed as dangerous, poisonous or hazardous to health.

Animals can learn some EQ through being tamed, and some go as far as becoming a companion animal. This is evident in pets' and zoo animals' behaviours and habits that have been cultivated through taming.

Tamed Fear

Accommodating Fear

We assimilate fear with the amygdala, just like animals do; this is why tamed animals are able to eat differently, react differently and interact differently from the vicious, untamed ones. This shows that one can remove the idea of fear without actually removing the amygdala. This is possible through training, awareness, and, sometimes, changing our perspectives and practices in regard to culture, religion, tradition, beliefs and lifestyle.

Changing our environment may also change our view, as does understanding other things, such as behaviours, actions, reactions or just basic interactions that exist outside our familiar ones.

Some things we do today to protect our existence, such as quick responses and development processes, are good innovations, solutions and protective measures that we may have cultivated through our perception, reactions and our behaviours. Some examples of these are the accident-and-emergency (A&E) services, the Google search engine, the police services, mobile phones (not smart phones), clocks, timers, alarms, education, artificial intelligence (AI),and augmented reality (AR) technology improvements, when seen as products, systems and services created to enhance our daily lives. These make us more effective without causing any defective behaviour, and can be seen as resulting from more-enhanced survival decisions.

When we are irrational, it is known to be resulting from a half-processed reaction, but when we process information properly and react more constructively, we are seen and known to be rational in our decision-making, or we are believed to have a more desirable reaction to the circumstances surrounding us. This is because rational decisions are associated with reasoning or a logic-based decision process, which relates more to intelligent thinking rather than emotional thinking. Our rational reaction could also be deemed to be more thinking out of the box or away from the norm, which is more critical to producing a good quality result.

Growing Fear

Rational thinking allows one to question every process and every possible outcome, in order to gain insights and understanding as to why an event has occurred. Rational thinking gives a well-thought-through reaction or non-action for an optimum level of beneficial and useful results.

Knowing that we are born with fear (i.e. it is innate), it is okay to say that we are born with irrational minds, or we could say that we are irrational beings, but that perfect imperfection gives us the ability to know that it is possible to keep growing and be better at decision-making without feeling imperfect.

This was also the topic of research conducted by Daniel Kahneman and Amos Tversky in the 1970s, which clearly concludes that we are not rational creatures through our having "cognitive biases", which demonstrates that humans systematically make choices that defies logic (Olivia Goldhill, 2020). In the conclusion of this research, it is obvious that fear is seen as illogical. These scholars also reveal that it is often overlooked that our irrational behaviour can be a good thing.

Not being able to make a careful decision at first, due to our inability to weigh the facts, doesn't mean we can't do so at a later time, as the opportunity to redecide will allow for a better decision to be made.

Illogical Logic of Fear

Consistently narrow self-interest

The Logic of Fear

Fear is illogically logical. In essence, fear can be rational, but the action or reaction to fear is what shows irrationality.Although rationality is never fully understood, our EQ understands, whilst our IQ rationalises and responds appropriately, as expected or as wanted.

A play on the name *Homo sapiens* (meaning wise man) creates the term *Homo economicus* (meaning economic man). *Homo economicus* portrays us humans as people who consistently have a narrow self-interest. We are optimistic people who are only trying to look after our subjectively defined results. The name *Homo economicus* suggests it's every man for himself.

Our behaviour is seen and assumed to be perfectly rational in the way it brings about an optimised, subjective good. Focusing on rationality, we can also say that fear is the only real feeling that shows our actual intent, but our rational behaviour, when seen as logical, can also be selfish (self-protecting) and narrow-minded, based on our past experiences, environment, mentality, exposure, age, gender, etc.

On the flip side, our irrational reactions or behaviour, which is said to be connected more with our emotional thinking than our intelligence, can be associated with an unreasonable, illogical or baseless decision process. These irrational reactions demonstrate inconclusive cognitive (first-hand view point) thinking, talking and action. This can almost be said to be an emotional or cognitive deficiency.

Our perception of emotional deficiency is a presumptuous thought that regards irrationality as an action or reaction that comes about through the inadequate use of reasoning. This presumption is quite demeaning to say the least, especially now that we know fear is seen as irrational, based on the neurological receptor (amygdala).

Our irrational thinking sometimes doesn't allow us to question every process and every possible outcome in order to gain insights and understanding as to why an event has occurred. It also naturally doesn't give us a well-thought-through reaction, but it can be more beneficial and useful in the end.

It is said that being irrational means not listening to reasons, logic or even common sense.

Our irrational behaviour can be laser-focused in fulfilling a need, and it might not change until that need has been fulfilled. That laser-focused behaviour, which is seen as irrational, can be unpredictable and sometimes dangerous.

It is difficult sometimes to think things through when we are experiencing fear, and so we respond instantly. This is quite natural.

We fight, flee or even protect ourselves, just like armadillos, pangolins and hedgehogs.

Fear Rationale

Fulfil a need

Armadillos

Armadillos claw at their attackers or threats. They leap vertically when startled, and when captured, they react by playing dead, either by stiffening or relaxing, but remain perfectly still either way. This is fear displayed through protection, which we would sometimes as humans, but can we conclude that the protection displayed here is an irrational reaction? This is a question to answer after the moment of fear has subsided, when armadillos don't feel threatened anymore, and they will open up and relax.

Pangolins

Pangolins have protective, large, keratin scales covering their skin, and they are the only known mammals with this feature. Pangolins can be bulletproof, and these armour scales around their body enhance their protective behaviour against attacks from larger animals. When pangolins feel threatened, they roll into a ball and use their scales as tough outer armour. This armour grows out of their skin, and it is shed regularly and replaced, as they grow and throughout their lives.

This type of protective action is effectively the armadillos displaying fear, and can be compared to the actions of some of us when we shield ourselves from harm through our reactions. The pangolins' reaction protects them naturally without needing any further measures in any sudden change of environment, and pangolins would probably not be able to understand a non-threatening environment because their natural protective behaviour is their default.

Can we say that the protective reaction of a pangolin is irrational at the moment of fear? Or can we say that this is a deficiency in the pangolins' behaviour? No, it is a protective and survival measure that is needed for them to stay alive. Why then do we think that our cultivated human-protective behaviours, which are comparable to these scenarios, are emotional deficiencies?

Hedgehogs

From a certain perspective, Hedgehogs could be seen as pets; they are quiet, quite active and entertaining. They also like being alone, but, in their defence, this is to avoid fighting with other hedgehogs. However, hedgehogs can be dangerous as their quills can penetrate the skin, and they have been known to spread bacteria and germs that cause fever, stomach pain and rashes. Hedgehogs love being held, but hugging a hedgehog might not be a good idea, as that could physically harm both parties due to the hedgehog's sharp quills.

Hedgehogs also protect themselves with their spines when attacked, and they are respected by others who understand their strong point of defence. Through understanding the features of this reaction, it can be seen to be a display of fear, even though there could be grounds for a mutually loving relationship.

Hedgehogs already understand threatening and non-threatening environments, and they have adjusted themselves in character for others to understand their actions in case the others come closer to them.

Our emotional reactions in fear sometimes make us look bad, even in a mutually loving environment, because our default reaction only protects us and might hurt others around us. Understanding our own behaviours and communicating these behaviours to others in a mutually loving environment is the key to protecting our loved ones as well as us in order to sustain that loving environment.

Fear Dominance

The common ground

Our fear actually begins with us as *Homo economicus* beings and, later, finds common ground with others around us, if we allow it.

Our fears subconsciously contribute to our association, culture, tribe, etc. that we find ourselves in, as well as other contributing factors that allow and initiate these entities. It is also possible for others to choose not to have common ground with us if they decide they don't want to be identified with us. Most times, this has nothing to do with our own fear, but it is instead based on the fears that others might be facing, which can only be understood by the people within their environment.

Fear of death used to be common ground for many, but, as we have evolved, religion or lack of it, culture, education, environment and exposure have changed people's understanding of their fears, and some have been able to tame their fear.

For example, lions and leopards are known to be vicious and predatory animals. A lion is described as the king of the jungle; it is a muscular, deep-chested cat with a rounded head, round ears and a hairy tuft at the end of its tail. It is also said that leopards are outstandingly strong, and they do kill humans when they are provoked or when they mistake humans for other animals. With this small amount of information, one is taught to fear lions and leopards, and if one is not in a position to kill either of the two, one should be ready to run for cover.

This is terrifying enough information to know, but, as we have evolved, our first step in dealing with that fear is creating awareness, educating ourselves and learning from all sort of experiences. As the dominant species, we have been successful in capturing, feeding and bringing these vicious predators to games for exhibitions, whilst creating a safe and secure habitat for these animals. We have also created safe, secure and friendly cohabitation for ourselves, as we reassure ourselves and take dominance from our intelligence.

Furthering this move to conquer or deal with our fear in this context, some people have upped their game by keeping these tameable creatures as pets, whilst they also use them to protect themselves from intruders and other threatening situations, and some use these animals to intimidate others and inflict fear for their own benefit.

The point here is that fear can be understood, fear can be tamed, fear can become strength and fear can be a form of protection. The approach to do this is encompassing every factor influencing fear into "perspective"; our perspective of fear influences our reaction automatically, and this is what changes results.

It is quite intriguing to see that we understand those with strength in our environment, we have researched and acknowledge all coexisting endangered and dangerous species in that environment through fear and experience. We have also created a world that accommodates these creatures, bringing them closer to our own habitat for diverse reasons, yet we see fear as weakness in other humans like us, who are either endangered or dangerous. We create cages for people like us who are probably reacting just like everybody else, without any understanding of how we can help them cohabit efficiently, whilst they improve themselves psychologically and physically, but we have found some sort of solace in demonising them for being human and ridding them of their weaknesses.

This illustrates that we create our own fear and choose how we deal with those fears; sometimes, we make excuses for the fear we shouldn't have in the first place and justify our action, reaction or lack of it for reasons only known to and benefitting us. This behaviour in itself is a weakening fear that causes resistance, xenophobia, discrimination turned into racism and other demeaning behaviours. We have been able to justify our fears, and direct our attacks and criticism straight into other environments, tribes, cultures, religions, beliefs and practices that aren't familiar to us.

Nothing causes fear more than a weakening fear.

Creative Fear

Effects of all possible reactions

When we are in fear, we are in our utmost creative realm. We somewhat understand that this is when we are most productive, either for ourselves, our immediate environment or a wider one.

Whilst we are learning more and understanding fear at all its levels, the reasons for our reactions and the phases of our fears, it will be good practice to channel our fear productively, humanely, logically and ethically. Thinking wider and beyond ourselves, seeing the bigger impact of all possible reactions or lack of them, and assessing which is the best result before taking steps to create a solution is a good thing.

As they say," heavy is the head that wears the crown"; we, as people, are a higher species compared to others that are known to exist, and no creature has been named without our knowledge and understanding. This level of capability may have required a lot of sacrifice, looking back in history, and, now that we have evolved, it will be even more evolutionary to use our fear to make things better, rather than creating more fear to promote our relevance.

We dwell at and have mastered the information (fear) stage, and we respond just as we feel a lot of the time and then think later. This is very normal. It is not a deficiency, as assumed, but completing the thought process will be good practice moving forward.

Fear, anxiety, trauma and insecurities are all part of us as humans. As stated previously, our reactions will need to be communicated, either through changing our perspective; interacting with our fears, without thinking of them as the weakness they have been deemed to be; and simply allowing others and/or our environment to acclimatise to our fears. This should give us better results.

Fear has no age restriction, as we have been made to believe. When we do not deal with our fears at any given stage, we will only grow with them, and we will accumulate more as we grow and evolve in other stages and phases of fear.

Fear is unlimited and inevitable; the more we fear, the more we fade.

Part of being mature or being responsible is revealed in how we deal with our fears; this is also why some believe that fear is a form of weakness, as they believe that some fears shouldn't exist in us once we have grown past certain stages of life. Whilst we can acknowledge this as a fact or a useful truth, we should also note that some of the fears that we had when we were young or younger can be brought back to us when we get older, and if those fears can be used against us, it almost becomes blackmail, or some sort of tool to get us to comply, act or react as wanted.

Authority is one of those fears that can be brought to us again and again at different stages of life.

Fear Redefined

The same fear that births anxiety can also cure it

Most of our design solutions, regulations, policies, etc. are done at this stage where fear is redefined. Politics may fit into this as well, as may revolution if we investigate these things properly and check the motives for them.

Fear and its meanings are used in different environments to achieve goals. Our fears can also become a lifestyle that directs our path throughout our whole life. Fear can crush confidence, but fear can also build confidence. Fear can cause illness, but fear can heal sickness and reduce pain. Fear can change minds, and fear can force hands. Fear can cause us to make mistakes, but fear can prompt us to rectify mistakes. Fear can be responsible. The same fear that births anxiety can also cure it.

Fear, in layman's terms, is defined as an unpleasant emotion caused by the threat of danger, pain or harm. (Lexico.com, 2020) This is a simple definition of fear. Another definition says it is a distressing emotion aroused by impending danger, evil, pain, etc., whether the threat is real or imagined; it is the feeling or condition of being afraid (dictionary.com, 2020), so it maybe a fear of heights or being in awe of something. A third definition states fear is a feeling of anxiety concerning the outcome of something or the safety of someone (Lexico.com, 2020). A fourth definition says fear is the likelihood of something unwelcoming happening (Rebecca B.L Robinson, 2018). A final definition calls fear the mixed feeling of dread and reverence (Lexico.com, 2020).

In psychology, fear is seen as the psychology of phobias or, more simply, a phobia is where fear is perceived as a negative response.

Other words with meanings synonymous to fear are terror, horror, panic, anxiety, agitation, dismay, distress, worry, uneasiness, nervousness, etc. All these seem more like phobia reactions and an after-effect of the feeling of fear.

A phobia is defined as an extreme or irrational fear of or aversion to something (Jessica Truschel, 2020). A phobia relates more to our cultivated pattern of responses or reactions to the fear of something or the unknown. There are many ways phobias have been defined, classified, generalised or diagnosed, to categorise all our emotional reactions under a single term to assist with understanding, research, academic study and/or a solution or treatment path for that phobia.

Phobia and Fear

Perception and Behaviour

Looking at the details of some selected common phobias we may come across could help us better our understanding of phobia reactions.

Acarophobia

Acarophobia is an *extreme fear* of insects causing itching (Hitbullseye, 2020). Someone suffering from acarophobia will react by showing the symptom of itching.

Although insects are insects, they have to live, feed and thrive too, but the idea of them living on our skin is frightening enough to make someone feel a sense of danger, anxiety and panic. The thought of insects being around can also have a psychological effect on people with acarophobia.

Knowing an insect is near is terrifying for people with acarophobia. Feeling an insect crawling on their skin without sucking on their blood makes someone with acarophobia crazy. The actual painful feeling of being bitten or having their blood sucked destroys the mind of a person with acarophobia. The fear of itching or the fear of an insect that causes itching is also simply horrifying for those who have acarophobia.

It is also highly likely for people with acarophobia to just scratch and touch their skin sporadically, in fear of insects possibly crawling on their skin.

Whether they suffer from acarophobia or not, some people actually coexist with insects and understand how to respect them. They probably ignore the idea of insects on their skin and just use insect-repellent herbs that provide protection.

People with acarophobia have been known to have a psychological fear that makes them itch and scream just from seeing insects in their vicinity without actually being in contact with any insect.

Acrophobia

Acrophobia is an *extreme fear* or irrational fear of heights, floating, falling, or being injured or killed as a result of a fall from a height.

This is the one we all accept as a natural and non-discriminatory fear that may or may not be diagnosed. We recognise this phobia and deal with it at different stages of our growth. Some ignore it and don't see it as a problem, and others manage it throughout their life time.

It is known that some people get other illnesses, such as a stroke, whilst trying to deal with their phobia.

Other phobias related to acrophobia are bathophobia, which is an abnormal and persistent fear of depth, or the fear of falling from a high place into something like a deep, dark pool of water, a river or a staircase; batophobia, which is the fear of being close to tall or big structures, such as mountains and skyscrapers; and climacophobia, which is the fear of the act of climbing.

It can be said that we all suffer from acrophobia, bathophobia and batophobia at some point or another in life, and some just never try to understand it due to it being accepted and knowing that it doesn't really have a treatment process, but is more a case of increasing our awareness as we evolve.

Aerophobia

Aerophobia is diagnosed as an *abnormal or irrational and persistent fear* of flying, fresh air or draughts. It could be as a result of personal experiences of sounds from storms or tornadoes, and their strength and capabilities when they occur. It could also be from other environmental factors, culture, religion, association, exposure and/or witnessing other people's experiences.

This phobia reaction could be seen to be a safety measure from the patients' perspective at first, but it later becomes a clear avoidance of adventures that could involve flying, jumping, gliding or being in the midst of stormy winds.

Aerophobia is quite similar to acrophobia, but specific to flying, and the sound of wind, storms and tornadoes.

The good news is that there are other ways of doing things until the people with this phobia are able to face and manage their fear, or until there are no alternatives to getting things done. It also is good to know that aerophobia is sometimes not known to the people with aerophobia until they experience flying, though some people end up suffering paralysis or a stroke after the experience.

If aerophobia is not discovered and treated immediately, as an after-effect of a flying, storm or tornado experience, it can become a lifelong illness, and has also been diagnosed as hereditary.

Agoraphobia

Agoraphobia is explained as *an extreme or irrational fear* of entering open or crowded places; leaving one's safe, familiar and controlled spaces, such as one's home; or being in places where escape is seen to be difficult.

Agoraphobic reactions could be influenced by experience, environment, exposure or lack of it, culture, age, sometimes guilt and most times just personal exposure (mobbing and intervention are examples of being personally exposed to appropriate situations).

There are major environmental factors that trigger agoraphobia in people. When we misunderstand certain characters due to their interaction skills or lack of them, their dress sense, their language, their approach to processes, their sense or level of understanding and their behaviour; we may drive them to agoraphobia. Once a person feels this way, they may begin to isolate themselves, become quiet or avoid certain social gatherings.

Agoraphobic behaviour or reactions could also be misdiagnosed without having a full understanding, and could end up in other damaging circumstances and other phobias than were bargained for. Most agoraphobic people don't know why they are the way they are, and may not be able to communicate this, as their agoraphobia only occurs when their safe environment is compromised.

Some people around agoraphobic people just see them as having unapproachable problems (i.e. having a problem in that they cannot be approached) and ignore them when these "defects" occur.

People with agoraphobia will avoid going anywhere they are unsure of, situations that may bring attention to themselves, may cause anxiety, or may trigger resentment, panic or other behavioural issues when they feel trapped, helpless or embarrassed. Agoraphobic people can create pockets of safe environments and will travel anywhere for that safe environment.

Those with agoraphobia are not always extremely reactive to the environment of fear, but can be negatively responsive to the people and objects in that environment as a form of reaction.

Apparently, exposure treatment or therapy (intervention) can cure this condition, and some have been prescribed certain medications. However, many find it difficult to overcome their phobia because the treatment environment and the short-lived medication could also add to their existing phobia. It has to be treated case by case, and a general treatment pack cannot be prescribed.

Some personal strategies are also recommended as a way to stop a panic attack, which might work in this context, such as deep breathing, recognising that one is having a panic attack, closing one's eyes, practising mindfulness, finding a focus object, using muscle relaxation techniques or picturing a happy place. However, this will mean that other people are aware of what is going on, which is impossible in most unknown environments and all these recommendations bring unwanted or unpleasant attention to the patient and could cause more harm (embarrassment, misjudgement, aggravation, bullying or helplessness) than good in the long run.

Although it is not age restricted, agoraphobia is common amongst teenagers, professionals, religious people, immigrants, criminals, those with different sexual orientations, those who have experienced abuse, shy people, some of the rich and famous, some people with disabilities, and people with post-traumatic stress (PTS) or post-traumatic stress syndrome (PTSS).

Agyiophobia

Agyiophobia is the fear of busy streets or crossing a busy street. This may or may not be related to agoraphobia through exposure and from unknown environments. It could be caused by a traumatic experience, and could be influenced by history, age or genetics. The symptoms are usually anxiety, dread and panic.

Aichmophobia

Aichmophobia is described as an *abnormal or disturbing fear* of sharp things, such as pencils, needles, knives, pointing fingers, the sharp end of an umbrella, or any sharp edges and corners of objects personally deemed to be dangerous.

This is very disturbing and could be caused by traumatic experiences, and influenced by the environment, exposure, information, culture, history and fiction.

People with aichmophobia are worried constantly and fearful about getting stabbed, not just intentionally but even by accident, and so they overreact in places with sharp objects, and try to tuck the objects away in case of any accidents or bad intentions.

Those suffering from aichmophobia may also run to get sharp objects when they feel threatened and may hold them for protection, but they do not always intend to use them knowing what damage they might cause. However, you never know what could happen in such circumstances, so it might be best to find a way to treat this phobia for the general protection of everyone.

Ailurophobia

This is diagnosed as an *extreme and irrational fear* of cats attacking, staring at and touching the person in question. Ailurophobia is caused by having a personal experience of being attacked by a cat or witnessing a cat attacking someone else at a young age. These factors are environmental and historical.

This type of phobia gets better as one matures, but it might not be a good idea for someone with this phobia to cohabit with a cat.

Sometimes a fear of wild cats, such as lions and leopards, may be extended to pet cats due to their similar features and behaviour.

Algophobia

This is an *abnormal and persistent fear* of anticipated pain. The pain caused by the fear is far more agonising than the actual pain that is inflicted.

This type of phobia could have been learnt and cultivated from a culture of pain, where one makes a certain exaggerated sound of being in pain to exert the culture and make people aware of the current event.

Without undermining the pain that women go through during childbirth, this is an example where every woman is told about the excruciating pain that comes from the delivery process. Whilst some women give birth without a single scream, some look for medication and solicit a pacifier through medication. Others request a caesarean section as an alternative in order to avoid the painful process. This is not to say that there is no pain in childbirth, but showing this phobia may create a culture of fear, and, as in the definition of algophobia, it can be said that it describes specifically a culture of pain.

As seen in other similar phobias, people who have certain phobia tend to end up virtually experiencing it. People with algophobia tend to suffer pain regardless of the fear, because the pain is anticipated, and so the pain is already being felt psychologically.

Another example is the fear of syringe needles (piercing pain), where the patient witnesses the process of filling the syringe with liquid, knowing that it will later be administered into their skin. This process causes the patient to anticipate excruciating pain before the actual injection, after which the pain not experienced becomes embarrassing enough to keep the patient acting as if they are in pain.

Amaxophobia

Amaxophobia is the *fear* of riding in a motorised vehicle at a speed or manner classified as unsafe by the patient. It develops as a result of experience, history, background, exposure, education, environment, religious doctrinal beliefs or a panic attack relating to the surrounding objects and the anticipation of unpleasant circumstances. This relates directly to the fear of getting into an accident, which might lead to pain, discomfort, loss or death.

There is always a first time for everything, but letting first-hand experience create a pattern of behaviour can be damaging.

Amaxophobia may also lead to or develop into vehophobia, which is an intense and persistent fear of driving a vehicle. This is a major problem for a lot of people who have experienced or witnessed a car accident, and the fear of being in one makes them avoid being behind the wheel. Vehophobia may also develop as a result of our background, exposure, education and religious doctrinal beliefs.

The funny thing about people with amaxophobia or vehophobia is that, once they have conquered their phobia of being in a moving vehicle or learn how to drive, they may turn out to be the most careful drivers, the most careless ones or a passenger who is a backseat driver, due to their eye for detail and their strong hazard-perception skills.

The idea of "once bitten, twice shy" validates fear. This doesn't mean that one never does something again, but rather that wisdom and understanding are applied to any repeat experiences.

Fear forms a culture, and we all understand what obstacles are, but once we feel there might be a hindrance in our process of achieving something, and we see that as life threatening, we do not wait to assess the possibilities; we assume that there aren't any other options but to quit.

Sometimes, we confuse our fear with fate.

Anthropophobia or Anthrophobia

Anthropophobia or anthrophobia is the *fear* of people (Jaime R. Herndon, 2018). It is more of a fear of interpersonal relations than the fear of a physical human figure. It is a culture-specific concept of distress that has been observed in Japan and Korea. It is almost like avoiding confrontation or not wanting to offend others around one.

We can almost compare anthropophobia to social anxiety disorder, or agoraphobia and agyiophobia, which are the fear of being in a crowd and the fear being in open spaces, respectively, but they are not totally the same.

The aspect of this phobia that refers to avoiding of people focuses on confrontation, conversations and aggravation that might be offensive to others. It is the action that spells out what the phobia might be.

Each of these three correlating phobias mentioned may be mistaken for another of the three when one does not ask the right questions or when the appropriate procedures are not followed.

A person with social anxiety disorder feels an uncontrollable fear of being judged or rejected by other people, and they may often avoid social spaces and events altogether when they can, for their own peace of mind. However, anthropophobia can also include symptoms that are totally unrelated to social interaction.

We have evolved to the point where we are brave enough to have social interactions, even though we don't want to, and, in most cases, we do so when we are pressured and compliant to our culture, environment and religious beliefs. This behaviour sometimes helps us to deal with our phobia, and it is not necessarily a bad thing, as long as we are able to find some happiness in the end.

Xenophobia

Xenophobia is described as the *fear* of strangers; the dislike of or prejudice against people from other countries; or the fear of other races, cultures, ways of life and people dissimilar to oneself.

Interestingly, xenophobic reactions can cause social anxiety disorder, agoraphobia and agyiophobia in an environment where people avoid confrontation, being judged or rejected.

Fear may defend itself by causing further fear, which is a defence that is justified in itself. The actual fear and reaction of those with xenophobia stems from an innate fear, and it is anthropophobic, agoraphobic and agyiophobic in nature. The only difference is the "justified" reaction of fear, which isn't partial avoidance or running away but fighting and defending oneself through violence, passive aggression, intimidation, false accusation, prejudice, discrimination, deprivation, competition, etc. The justification for this excuse for xenophobia is that the unidentified, unusual and unfamiliar presence of strangers threatens the sufferer's own existence, and there is a need to eradicate the foreigners to protect sufferer's own interests; i.e. land, jobs, infrastructure, facilities, benefits, family and their own people.

What is seen to be hate in xenophobia is actually fear in action and reaction.

Xenophobia in itself can be cultural, political or ethical. Xenophobic behaviour can be cultivated, developed and passed on from generation to generation, as a tradition, rule of law, legislation or regulation, way of life or policy. Xenophobia may also become a practice of racial stereotyping, a belief, an instinctive reaction or a perspective for some.

Xenophobic behaviour is the complete opposite of xenophilia, which is an attraction to foreign people. Xenophilia sometimes is an over-compensation of past xenophobic behaviour due to the evolution of one's character. We could call xenophiles "sympathisers" because they have decided to celebrate or appreciate the difference in others that used to be resisted.

Anglophobia

Anglophobia, which is the *fear* of England or the English, also fits into the category of xenophobia, and it causes intimidation, discrimination and an inferiority complex for the non-English people.

The counter-reaction of fear may be damaging, and, today, the idea of supremacy exists in the mind of Anglophobic people as a counter-reaction more than the belief that the English imposed authority in England's history of colonialism.

Without undermining the impacts or the effects of all sorts of atrocities of colonialism, it has been told as a different kind of tale, which has been demonstrated through brutality, injustice, prejudice, xenophobia and racism, when, in actual fact, the real problem is just a subjective fear that has caused alarm, and been falsely reflected and portrayed to other people.

With full acknowledgement of the psychological effects of all the problems caused by these phobias from all parties, it is also necessary to know the root cause of some beliefs and deal with the problems directly, rather than blaming the other possible contributory factors.

Some global organisations have been set up to promote diversity and bring corporate governance to certain continents. For example, the European Union (EU) brings together people of different languages, cultures, beliefs and practices to create liberty and a corporate policy for the benefit of the European countries (which before Brexit included France, Germany, United Kingdom (UK), Spain and other European countries) for common regulation, free trade, free movements, education and other reciprocated benefits.

It is also known that some of these participating countries are seen as more powerful, influential and humanitarian than others. These powerful and more influential participating countries are also in the front line for consultation and advice due to their exposure, economic strength and accomplishments. This level of leadership comes with its burdens, and these burdens may sound and look unequal, unfair and a total abuse of the union.

The leading countries and their people may see themselves as privileged and seen by the other vulnerable participating countries as the supreme entities to call on when bail outs and aid are needed.

A typical example in this case is the United Kingdom (UK), which, prior to Brexit, was seen as a strong participating country that could bail others within EU out of an economic crisis and the country that mainly supplied much of the aid to the EU. This is an extra burden or responsibility when it comes to trade, immigration and other home-country facilities being shared with all other EU countries, whilst the UK and its people struggled to gain any benefits in their own country. The process, policy and access of the British citizens to their own benefits and facilities in the UK became more tedious and scrutinised compared to the process the citizens of other EU countries go through when they are in the UK.

Funnily enough, the British people thrive regardless of these benefits, and are able to live much better in some of the EU countries than the citizens of those benefiting countries themselves. This is due to the supreme way the British are perceived and treated in some of the EU countries.

The idea of Anglophobia works in the favour of English people without any effort, due to the perception of the non-English. This un-imposed reverence puts non-English under the control and influence of the English people. This shows that a phobia gives in psychologically to fear and allows itself to be controlled by the fear because it believes that the fear is supreme to it. Anglophobic people may also give into their fear through compliance, obedience and trust, and be led into being controlled by the English. Of course, would any people group say no to reverence, good attention, lordship, success and control being handed over to them at no cost or fault of their own? If that were you, would you not take advantage of the situation?

In the past, English have obviously taken full advantage of the situation for their own benefit, and so blaming, shaming and persecuting the English for a situation that they did not cause is unproductive and unfair. Blaming and shaming the English will also not change the situation, as the action is focused in the wrong direction.

Fear self-imposes an un-imposed reverence; it allows itself to be controlled and influenced by its perception. It is still an outstanding question today as to why hundreds of slaves were able to obey and comply with the rules of only one master in a massive plantation back in the times of the mass slavery of Africans. It is now more obvious that the fear that existed in the slaves at that time was a reverence rather than the simple fear of the outcomes of being resistant to their masters. This reverence had built some psychological trust, which believed that the English slave master was more intelligent, knew better, lived better and would give a better life to others if only they would stay loyal, committed and fully comply with the rules and regulations set by the English.

Fear convinces itself that it is doing the right thing for the greater good.

When we are in fear, it is quite possible for us to submit completely without any resistance, thought or feelings of being violated. This behaviour is a psychological side effect of our fear. When we are in fear, we can become an ally to our oppressor, protecting their interests, paying them homage and carrying out their wishes without asking for anything in return, and also without feelings of being oppressed, frightened, controlled or persuaded to do anything we don't want to do.

Fear confuses compliance and submissiveness with loyalty, and somehow it feels powerful in submission. It is confident that its interests are protected through its deluded belief in its principles being justified.

Francophobia

Francophobia or Gallophobia is another phobia related to xenophobia, which is defined as *fear of, strong dislike of, or prejudice against* France, the French or the French culture. We may also explain it as anti-French sentiment, which is an *extreme or irrational* fear or contempt of France, the French, the French government or the Francophones (French-speaking political entities who use French as an official language or whose French-speaking population is larger than others in the district).

Our history and personal experiences, combined with our brain chemistry, genetics and heredity play a major role in the development of certain phobias we may have.

Based on our case studies so far, we can say that Francophobia and Anglophobia probably have the same effect on people. Some of the facts that we have discovered about Anglophobia mostly also relate to Francophobia, but, for some mentalities and perceptions, it is also known that our phobia or fear may manifest through resistance, hate or a strong dislike.

The fear that causes resistance, hate or strong dislike are strongly suggestive enough to give people with Francophobia or Anglophobia a reason to want to eliminate, destroy, capture, colonise or change the French or English culture, respectively.

Another reason for the reactions born out of Francophobia and Anglophobia is the belief that Western culture and its people are misleading, misdirecting and hypnotising the world in many subjectively unethical ways, and the need to change the West's ways and adjust its culture, teachings, leadership and principles for the better is a must and the ultimate goal.

Russophobia

Russophobia is a *strong dislike, intense and often irrational hatred* towards Russia and Russian things, especially the political system or custom of the former Soviet Union.

Russophobes clearly and explicitly direct their hate, dislike or irritation at the policies, entities, leadership, practices and things around the system that represents Russia rather than a fear or frightened reaction towards a Russian person or people. However, Russophobia may be extended to and reflect on Russians if care is not taken.

A typical example of Russophobia is the removal of Russia from the G8 Summit, which is an annual meeting between leaders from eight of the most powerful countries in the world, whose aim is to manage common problems by discussing and planning actions for global growth. The country of Russia was removed from the G8 Summit, which then became the G7 Summit, due to the Crimean crisis involving Russia and Ukraine, in addition to other underlying political and global security issues.

We sometimes extend our fear reaction towards certain practices, entities, polices and things surrounding them to other non-participating members, citizens of the district, country or entity, just because we have psychologically categorised everything and everyone relating to those practices, policies or entity as part of the unit. When we say, "birds of a feather flock together" or when we say, "bad company corrupts good character," we mean and feel the same way about anything and everything that is related with the subject.

Russia is still under a lot of scrutiny to date at the time of writing, and there are more fears and resulting diplomatic activities to reduce Russia's influence and interference in political events in other countries.

Fear has somehow related Russophobia with Anglophobia and Francophobia, as a culture with different subjective, unethical practices that are seen as unacceptable by others in fear; i.e. Russophobes, Anglophobes and Francophobes.

Phobias Between Western Countries

Countries with a Western culture may also work against each other and develop some form of phobia towards each other, due to endless possible causes of fear; e.g. culture, practices, territory, possessions, immigration and history.

A good example of this is the long-standing history of hostility and conflict between England and France dating way back to the eleventh century. The anti-French sentiment in Britain has portrayed France as an oppressive, poverty stricken and backward culture. Religion, culture, nationalism, colonialism and supremacy have played a major role in the rift between the two countries, causing resentment and resistance against France.

The ideas causing the French Revolution that emerged thereafter were totally feared and not received well by the British monarchy and monarchists.

The rest of the countries on the European continent were also resistant to the French Revolution due to its possible spread impacting the legitimacy of the hereditary monarchy, and urban poor people and the uneducated peasants gaining power over their traditional social masters.

The French Revolution as a movement was also criticised for being anti-clerical, terrorising and not as liberating as expected. It also created more resistance, and more anti-French feelings in some of the people, their countries, their sayings, their practices and politics, creating more criticism for the actions of the French. The French colonial empires also gained a lot of enemies amongst their rival colonial countries and the colonised people. The French interference in other government policies and practices, their intervention in civil wars, and their collaborations with other colonies were also scrutinised and resented by the Africans and the Asians.

These resentments towards the France triggered anti-French violence in many countries, such as Ireland, Australia, New Zealand and the United States. As a sign of solidarity, the Chinese also executed some French marines as an expression of anti-French feelings.

Francophobia has been felt much more by the French, even though they were the feared, and the global fear here went beyond resentment, avoidance or being frightened, but it was expressed more through violence against the French people. Everything and everyone that represented that culture was also seen as an enemy.

The Francophobes, who were meant to feel fear, then chose to protect themselves, and to show resistance through violence and protest against France and everything French. They did this by eliminating French influences from their vicinity, and expressing territorial traits by and through execution and the removal of the French people and their culture.

Fear can be dehumanising, due to the perception and reaction of the people and things around us, and the end result of that fear makes us feel less human, gives us an inferiority complex and makes us feel victimised.

Fear loathes interference, intervention and criticism. These things irritate fear and build its resistant power to dehumanise though its reactions, and cause a concoction of fear due to the existence of different experiences, reactions and outcomes. When we are in fear, we naturally resist interference and criticism by other people around us, because it makes the feeling worse, and makes us fight back and resist all opinions and advice without thinking through the reasons behind all the interfering behaviour conducted by others around us.

Our reaction when in fear creates friction in our relationships with people and things around us, and this could be one of the reasons why some of us find it difficult to see some opportunities and great ideas around us.

Scopophobia or Scoptophobia

Scopophobia or scoptophobia is an anxiety disorder characterised by an *extreme fear* of being seen, stared at or stared down at. Scopophobia is also classed as the fear of being exposed, vulnerable, judged, criticised, hated, found irritating or unwanted, and, in some cases where attention is not being paid, it is seen as liking not being paid attention to.

All in all, scopophobia gives an uncomfortable feeling that needs to be understood before one reacts. The usual and general reaction to scopophobia is running away, being silent, being startled, having a non-functional state of mind, nervous smiles, giggling, blushing, staring back, frowning, making fists, fidgeting, developing a faster heart rate, compliant behaviour, shivering, being intimidating and avoiding eye contact. Those who suffer from scopophobia are triggered by having numerous anxious thoughts, which they might not wait to observe before reacting.

The other opposite of scopophobia is scopophilia, which is deriving sexual pleasure from watching others when they are naked or engaged in sexual activity. This is sometimes imagined and fantasised rather than physical or substantial.

Looking at the interaction between scopophobia and scopophilia, sometimes when people with scopophobia meet those with scopophilia who gaze lustfully, the outcome is offensive, abusive and can be controlling. Whilst the lustful gaze of those with scopophilia is purely for sexual pleasure, the people with scopophobia misunderstand completely and react to the gaze in one or more of the possible actions listed previously. Those with scopophilia may misinterpret the scopophobic reaction as reciprocated liking, and decide to take the interaction further by acting bravely, inappropriately or in an unwanted manner towards the person with scopophobia.

In all indications, a patient with scopophilia sees further than what is shown, and the gaze or body language of someone with scopophilia is all interaction with and communication of what's in their mind. They can apply images through experiences and those concocted in their imagination, then insinuate responses that are presumed to fit, and, finally, give an anticipated reaction to satisfy the urge.

Scopophilia is mostly genderised but not gender restrictive; they may misread a scopophobic reaction to be sexual and misbehave in reciprocation to satisfy the urge in an imagined sexual activity or interaction.

Fear misread as confidence makes someone the most attractive in the room to someone with scopophilia.

Our fear has shaped a lot of the unwanted relationships, friendships, leaderships and partnerships of all kinds that we may have found ourselves involved in, and, unfortunately, may have also caused more harm in many lives today.

Our miscommunication, interactions, and misinterpretation of our fears and other people's intentions towards us has really pushed us to the edge by suggesting the wrong reaction to us through our process of fathoming out our mental status, without giving us the time to digest what is being experienced.

Scopophobia may actually explain more about our phobias than it seems, because, when we are in fear, we are able to see ourselves only in that fear and visualise our condition in that fear before reacting to any suggested or anticipated result. The major issue here is that we don't take or have the time to process the situation properly before reacting.

A patient with a phobia is like a person with a third eye looking into themselves and seeing themselves as a victim of a circumstance who plans to take action to prevent the anticipated result. When we are in fear, we can literally see or imagine ourselves as another person, and almost imagine every possible outcome of our position and then take quickly the most likely action or reaction that is in our own interest.

Negrophobia

Negrophobia is the *irrational fear and irritating dislike* of black people. Allegedly, Negrophobes' thought of black people triggers anxiety and panic attack, depending on their genetics and environment.

Moving forward, we must acknowledge that Negrophobia is a psychological disease that has killed more people than any epidemic, pandemic, plague or continuously present disease such as malaria, which might have killed more than anticipated.

Negrophobia is one psychological illness that was not seen originally as a form of disease or any kind of psychological defect in those suffering from it. Throughout its existence, Negrophobia has been a gradual and progressively destructive disease that developed through the white colonial aggression into African slavery, the slave trade, discrimination and racism towards black people.

Segregation, incarceration, politics, supremacy, profiling, and some sports and recreational activities were made mainly to dehumanise black people. Abuse of many kinds, immigration, incentivised customs, and cultural policies and bills were also designed and passed for the less privileged, and the less privileged back in the day were mostly black people.

We can see all these in the link between Negrophobia and blackophilia, which is where white people or other coexist races, are fascinated by, are attracted to and consume black culture and the portrayed lifestyle that is mostly seen in things such as music, athletics, sports, drug use and drug dealing, continuous resistance, protests and movements that challenge institutions and constitutions that are deemed to be racist or racially motivated.

Negrophobia and blackophilia have become a naturally conditioned response where white people or people of other races are seen as having power or being powerful, and black people are seen as being powerless, so much so that superiority through power has been transferred subconsciously to white people or people of other races ruling black people.

Black people have been made to believe that they are not human but are irrational, emotional, aggressive wild animals, and must be colonised and controlled to make a better world. They have also been made to believe that being liberated is a privilege, and that a sense of gratitude should be the subconscious infection of the black race. This make-believe effort by white people or people of other races has since developed the idea of Negro-Negrophobia.

Negro-Negrophobia is a black mental disorder (delusion) generated from Negrophobia that transfers the hate, dislike and irrational fear of white people or people of other races to black self-disgust, black self-irritation, black self-sabotage, black self-dehumanisation and black self-fascinating fear. Basically, Negro-Negrophobia is a black person's mental disorder that makes them believe that they are not meant to exist as people or as a part of the human race.

The mentality of Negro-Negrophobia has generated some sense of guilt, a sense of responsibility and aspiration to be anything other than black. Negro-Negrophobia is also being incorporated with a motivation to change black mentality, personality and appearance to fit into the human race as portrayed through Negrophobia. Every other "successful" black person or statistically handpicked, upstanding black person sees themselves as a better or preferred individual in the pack and feels the need to become a mentor, a role model, a subject, a voice for change, or a representative of a feasible change and the acceptable appearance of blackness transformed.

This demonstrates that Negrophobia has grown to the point where even black people now suffer from the same illness, and the phobia has been transferred back to black people. They have now been brainwashed into believing that their kind is not good enough, and should either be destroyed, regenerated, rebred or changed.

Negro-Negrophobia turns black people into self-destructive beings, who believe that integrating white people or Western ideas, culture, lifestyle and standards into their own is a social and global advancement, and it shows growth. This makes black people desperate to integrate into white or Western systems, religion, communities, ideologies, movements and organisations, just so they are recognised, accepted and regarded as part of the evolving and developed or developing world.

Some black people would even gladly die in abandonment of their values to integrate in order to show they are different, so that they may be regarded amongst the black communities as being visible, intelligent, elite, Western, etc. Black people of this type are allegedly seen as possible leaders, entrepreneurs, speakers and the ones with the knowhow. Intriguing right?

Negro-Negrophobia has turned black people against each other, whilst doing the bidding of Negrophobia.

More Negrophobia exists today amongst black people who are meant to be the victims of the rhetoric of other races, and they now also hate their kind, dehumanise their kind, dislike and despise their kind, execute their kind, weaken their kind, enslave their kind, violate their kind, and build subcultures against their kind through ideologies of Negrophobia and blackophilia.

Fear is a major source of wealth and relevance.

Failure, poverty, weakness, labour, war, slavery, crime, violence (in music especially), ignorance and much more are the things that people who are Negrophobic will think first when they think of black people. The facial expressions of people who are Negrophobic, brought on by their thoughts about black people, mostly show irritation, and, in some other cases, a realisation of a source of wealth and relevance.

The appreciation, attraction and fascination of blackness in some others is an opportunity brought about through Negrophobia and blackophilia; this allows the building of businesses and contingencies to support these expressions, and creates opportunities as some sort of incentive for the victims to be compensated for their pain and suffering. This still lies within Negrophobia, as these people cash in on ignorance, illiteracy, labour, war, slavery, poverty and a lack of resources, and build their wealth around crime, regulations, black culture, needs and essentials, inflation, and violence.

Fear creates dominance and submission simultaneously.

The ability to coexist with black people who are feared can boost confidence and make white people or people of other races believe they will always thrive in the midst of all these atrocities, because black people are not smart enough to think for themselves or by themselves, ask the right questions, live independently or operate independently.

This is a big part of the supremacy movement that still exists today.

Our significantly scopophobic nature suggests that submissiveness as a reaction to fear also may have enhanced some of our suffering and maltreatment by others.

Negrophobia and Negro-Negrophobia are no different, except that Negrophobia was never seen as a phobia but as some form of leadership, control, and an efficient way to globalise and make the world a better place.

Fear is dehumanising and can dehumanise simultaneously due to perception, reaction, lack of reaction and results. The idea of discrediting our fear by perceiving it as being a state of some sort of weakness to be exploited is actually deluded and more dehumanising than anything else.

When we understand that our fears are innate, very natural and a part of our growth, as we create awareness, work through them and change our attitude towards our fears, we will activate our liberation, wisdom and courage to handle all our fears and get better results from them.

Negrophobia has brought about self-seeking aid, humanitarianism, trade, incentivised immigration laws and the creation of business to "develop" places seen as desolate, dark, ignorant, backward, helpless and isolated.

The supremacy movement only took over when potential for wealth and power was discovered and because fear, as seen with Francophobia, resists culture and practices, and creates hatred, which leads to execution, sanctions, dehumanisation, etc. We can see that Negrophobia has caused this and more.

An example of this is the idea of humanitarianism. Humanitarianism is the promotion of human welfare when the most vulnerable lack access to basic needs, such as food, shelter, health care and education. Humanitarianism brings aid to help meet those needs with the aim of saving lives, soothing/eradicating suffering, facilitating a better life and maintaining humanity.

Humanitarian effort is achieved through different means, doctrines and practices, but mostly religious practices. Some of our political practices have religious ethics behind them, and their morals have been built on religious grounds, and so a government's dignity and responsibilities towards its people are geared towards protecting and maintaining human dignity.

A humanitarian initiative is built around the needs of vulnerable people, communities, entities and largely countries. Such an initiative is really a good practice.

Looking at what we now know about certain human interactions and phobias, and understanding about the reactions of different cultures and practices, it is quite saddening to realise that most humanitarianism that exists is actually dehumanitarianism.

Phobia and Dehumanitarianism

Man the panic, Man the pill

Dehumanitarianism is the act of promoting the deprivation of positive human qualities and welfare, or employing prejudice and the support of human suffering for personal or collective institutional gain on the grounds of division (or divide and conquer).

This is fear in full reaction.

Sometimes, when we are in fear, we resist, resent and work against ourselves and our environment. We become controlling, spiteful, prejudiced, and support anything and everything that works against what we fear, although our actual goal is really to eradicate our feeling of fear. Sometimes when we are in fear, we couldn't care less about other people's quality of life and welfare, as long as our fear is suppressed and totally under our control. We undermine everything that supports or brings out the fear in us, just so that we can remove the feeling of fear.

The goal of dehumanitarianism is to control lives, finances, resources, trade, intercontinental relationships and governance through intimidation, sanctions, inflicting suffering, creating crises and supremacy, for personal and institutional gain.

Dehumanitarianism causes crises; creates vulnerabilities, a lack of resources and resistance; and then restricts access to basic needs, such as food, shelter, health care and infrastructure, in order to control governance, dictate provisions, and manipulate the allocation of help to meet needs based on compliance.

Although dehumanitarianism saves lives, it is done on its own terms and nothing less. Dehumanitarianism is not a dictatorship, but a subtle totalitarianism with a doctrine that promotes capitalism, modern slavery, earned human rights and complete classism.

Simply put, dehumanitarianism is the creation of a crisis to solve a crisis. Man the panic, man the pill.

Dehumanitarianism is a system fuelled by fear. We sometimes shed crocodile tears in fear to gain attention and moral support. We may also pretend or play dead in fear, just like armadillos and pangolins, when we feel threatened, and then strike viciously as soon we have certain assesses to what we fear in protection of ourselves.

Today, what is initiated in places in need is rather dehumanising, but it is seen as good practice.

Negrophobia is directed at individuals, organisations and entities belonging to black people, and black domains are seen both by those suffering from Negrophobia and other black people as undeveloped, desolate, dark places created as landfill due to the narrative that it produces chaos for the rest of the world. It is a better definition to say that Negrophobia is an irrational, dehumanising and fascinating fear, dislike and hate of black people.

All the theories around these kinds of phobia and mental disorders, including the resistance and reactions of irritation mentioned in this volume, may be acted upon in so many ways, including trade wars, civil wars, terrorism, xenophobia, discrimination, prejudice, violent protest, selective aid, alliances, global policies and ethics. The theories are also enacted in religious movements, other ethical beliefs, cultural beliefs, the deployment of weapons of mass destruction, immigration, business and trade affiliations, isolation, and sanctions.

These suggested reactions could be from a place of fear believed to be faith, or, more likely, a place of resentment, prejudice and judgement believed to be just.

Fear recognises difference as opposition, and will only refer and react to difference as being the opposite to itself. In a sense, our differences allow and embrace diversity that brings all of our cultures, orientations, personalities and experiences together to boost and transmit our multicultural, multi-denominational and multi-environmental values into one single space.

For some strange reason, our differences naturally hit us as being in opposition, or an opposite opinion, view, idea, belief, culture, orientation and personality, especially when we are in fear. We naturally meet and respond to these differences with an opposite reaction to protect our interests.

Opposing Fear

Anticipated outcomes

We sometimes find it difficult to see value in differences when we are in fear. We see our differences as being some strange and offensive entity at first, but when our differences are persistently intentional or when we are deliberate about the value in our differences, without being or seen to be intimidating or manipulating, we may become comfortable in acknowledging the differences and develop an accommodating reaction.

Even though we acknowledge a difference as what it is, we are also able to enjoy the value that comes through diversity and integrate without fear.

Our political practices, for example, are known today only for their values, which are mainly divided into two parts in any given country. In politics, the political party that carries the vote gains the majority and leads the country through its own administration; therefore, the leading party has the power to nominate and recommend administrators and representatives of the government in every relevant area of government.

The governing party will always refer to the other parties as the minority, and throughout the governing party's tenure, every law, piece of legislation and government practice mutually understood and agreed will be ruled and controlled by the governing party.

In most cases, there are conflicts of interest in governance due to the governing party's sole interest.

Today, politics and democracy have been divided by our political parties' values, through the fear of differences, when politics should clearly enhance democracy.

We sometimes resist assistance, partnership or a team effort from those we perceive as different when we are in fear. This is probably because we don't have enough trust that others will have our interests at heart and work with us to achieve the goals we may have set.

As is generally known, our phobia could be caused and triggered by our negative events we have witnessed in the past and our experiences with specific people, climates, races, genders, religions, tribes or cultures, environments, and principles and practices learnt.

When we look back at these lections of overwhelmingly scary types of phobia we have explored in this volume, we could probably end up with all kinds of afflictions and self-diagnoses that are not necessarily true, and give up on life due to the greater fear of anxiety and other unrelated problems from phobias.

Bearing all our fears and phobias in mind as we interact with each other in finding solutions to our problems and working on making ourselves feel some sense of safety in our environment, there is the chance of running into other people who have their own unrelated fears that they are dealing with whilst they interact with us. These people we run into may also react strongly or irrationally in their decision-making, based on the way we interact with them and them anticipating outcomes due to their own experiences from other unrelated events. This mis-interaction and misunderstanding between us and the other people involved may cause more resentment and resistance, leading to other unwanted results between us as people, and between the system and us. A typical example of misunderstanding and miss-interaction is profiling.

Phobia and Profiling

Victim of circumstances

Profiling in the context of fear could be defined as the act of inferring unknown information about a person based on known traits, or the act of suspecting or targeting a person on the basis of the observed, informed, assumed and presumed characteristics or behaviour for a premeditated reaction to achieve an anticipated outcome.

Profiling, in this context, simply explains the fear of the unknown. The approach to the unknown isn't really incomprehensible, it is more like the premeditated, presumed, assumed and anticipated possible-but-unpredictable direction of results. When we are in fear of the unknown, we naturally prepare to protect ourselves.

It is said that attack is the best form of defence. When we don't know what the outcome of an event might be, we assume and presume all sorts of theories about people's behaviour, which is sometimes based on our experiences and at other times is based on other opinions we hold about certain people. We then cover our backs with premeditations in anticipation of the unknown directions things might take. This could make us paranoid, suspicious, prejudiced and discriminatory even though we sometimes disagree with the conclusion about our behaviour when we profile people. We do this through incarceration, intimidation, defence, offence, antagonism and/or overreaction.

The profiling process requires records, history, presumptuous information and beliefs, with some briefed or debriefed understanding incorporated with possible accessorised reactions and outcomes. Therefore, it is a fallacy to claim that a situation we have already profiled and premeditated is surprising. We only say this to defend ourselves and protect our interests.

When we profile people in fear, we show signs of scopophobia. We see ourselves only in our fear, and visualise our condition in fear before reacting to our imagination. The profiling process is almost scopophobic in nature, except that it could be either a pre-emptive reaction or premeditated action depending on intent.

Sometimes, our scopophobic behaviour allows us to see ourselves with a third eye, looking into ourselves and seeing ourselves as the victim of circumstances, even though this might not be the case. This could happen to either party involved in any given event. The plan to take action to control the anticipated result could also be from any party involved. We can all think that we are the victim in any situation, and that we are justified in our actions and reactions to defend ourselves. The only issue here is that these facts will only matter as in a report or a statement at a later stage. That is the crucial point: it doesn't always need to end as a defence, a report or a witness statement.

Phobia Pandemic

Functionality justified

A fear doesn't have to be extreme or exaggerated for it to be diagnosed as a phobia. A phobic reaction can also be subject to the environment, and the reaction to fear doesn't always need to be dramatic for it to be diagnosed.

Our environment matters when we are in fear. It either encourages us to exaggerate our emotions in fear or teaches us to communicate more calmly to contain the situation. The environment may also help to determine the level of fear we may have, due to the way it reacts or interacts with us when we show signs of fear.

When we express the feeling of fear in our environment, we may be exposing ourselves to judgement and a wrongly presumed diagnosis of who we might be. It's like automatically sectioning a person with anorexia and giving them a sedative when all they need is food and understanding.

A phobic reaction is sometimes observed to be complete avoidance of stimuli, but, at times, patients with a phobia have no choice but to react when their phobia creeps up on them as a surprise.

When we are in fear, in any given environment and at any given time, our reactions are numerous. We might be disruptive, distractive, anti-social, confrontational, unruly, forgetful, resentful, argumentative, non-responsive or over-reactive. We may also show fear in other unrelated or unrecognised ways such that the people around us may not be able to ascertain or understand why we are reacting, and be confused about how to help us.

Some feelings of fear are just our growth process rather than a mental health illness that needs to be diagnosed and prescribed a treatment. When we don't understand that fear is part of our growth process; that our fears do improve with age or time, and that other mitigating treatment factors for our fear may either worsen our fear or undermine our emotions, we are stuck nursing sicknesses that doesn't even exist in us.

We might also end up with photophobia, which is the fear of phobias (i.e. the fear of our emotions and reactions connected with other major phobias and anxieties that are bound closely to other anxiety disorders we may have which generally trigger panic attacks) and living our lives on tip toes.

If we are not intentional about understanding our fears and ourselves, we may be inflicting more fear on ourselves than we can handle, and will live in anxiety and fearing things that haven't sprung up in us yet.

It is extremely difficult to separate or differentiate a phobia from a fear. The differentiation process is tedious, because most diagnoses –which are based on certain factors such as age, gender, culture, experience, neurological development and environment–, are just guidelines for questions and surveys to gain insight and not the actual means to separate phobia from fear.

Phobias lead to fear, and fear is phobic in nature. Our reactions to both may have been said to be distinct, but that narrative is not entirely accurate. All definitions and synonyms of fear sound very negative, but there are more positive effects of fear than the negative or irrational feelings when these feelings are properly explored, digested, understood and allowed to complete their course without any disruptive opinion.

An epidemic can be made into a pandemic through fear or a phobic reaction. Pathophobia or nosophobia, which is an irrational fear of contracting certain illness or disease, can cause us to have a panic attack. Our panic attack in that moment may send the wrong signal to the rest of the world, including other people with the same pathophobia, and cause social disruption regarding a geographically restrictive outbreak of an uncontrollable or unusual disease or virus.

Our reaction in real time is collectively accepted and replicated for a desired or anticipated result. This is what happens when the fear of economic loss, political status, regulations, policies, lives, and personal health and dignity is threatened. It is only fair to raise the alarm for collective help or awareness through an exaggerated method such as using scaremongering and taking major steps to show the seriousness of the narrative.

More often than not, our fears need attention, action and reaction, but this should never be a compromise on the sustainable effectiveness of solution. We cannot allow our fears to be used for other people's personal gain.

A pandemic being declared would require national or global responses, especially to raise awareness, including in locations that are unaffected by the pandemic, but the truth is that one size does not fit all when it comes to fear. Our fears are experienced in different ways, but what makes them sound and look similar is our reaction. Unfortunately, our responses to any illness or disease are generally the same everywhere, regardless of the possible location of the infection, how infectious it is and the effectiveness of its treatment.

Our behaviour can be motivated or influenced by our fear, and we are judged as to whether or not that fear is an acceptable reason or a mitigating factor for our behaviour. They say experience is the best teacher. When our experience of fear influences our behaviour in a way that gives us control in situations we may have seen before, our cultivated approach to other similar situations will continuously be based on our previous experiences and reactions in order to achieve the same result. We may replicate the same behaviour as before and expect a similar outcome when we witness other people in situations similar to our experience, forgetting that we are not the one in that situation.

It is possible that the outcome we expect may or may not be desirable or useful to other people or parties in that similar situation, and so our experience and approach to that situation could be seen as disruptive, irresponsible, overpowering, unhelpful, controlling or invading other people's business, and we may be penalised for such behaviour.

Even though our behaviour is motivated by our previous experience of a similar event, our justifiable behaviour might be unacceptable based on factors such as the environment, the people involved, the culture, our pattern of behaviour, our age, our gender, our orientation, our beliefs and the motivation for the event.

Respecting other people's fears in our environment without imposing ours on them is probably a good way to understand ours.

Our fear experiences can also be the motivation for our behaviour to improve ourselves.

We isolate ourselves sometimes because of our fear. Most times, we are defensive because we are afraid. We antagonise others both in and outside our environment because of our fear. We become controlling in our environment because of our fear, and we may also control other people's behaviour for the same reason. We may become overly intimidating by oppressing others due to our own fear. We manipulate our way into things, and we become experts in knowing and getting our way around things because we are afraid. We judge others for our own fear and isolate others for our own benefit.

As a matter of fact, fear is probably the most important reason for or factor in a lot of the things that we have designed. In the case of designing policies, regulations, legislation, products, other systems and services, fear is seen as a way of providing insights through research, needs to be discovered to identify design opportunities or better functionality and/or efficiency. These reactions are seen in some human factors in design, sustainability, recycling, changing administrative policies in governments, companies and entities in control of our environment.

We are constantly afraid of death, extinction, acts of God, human reactions and reactive behaviours that may cause changes to our environment, although, some reactive behaviours may be seen as proactive measures. We review our practices continually to comply with policies and regulations that keep us together as people, and we continue to evolve our processes to reduce failures and inefficiencies in our products, systems and services.

Every unusual event or outbreak that occurs is an opportunity for new laws, new regulations, new designs, new processes, new systems, and new or newly integrated functions.

This behaviour makes it clear that we are growing in fear as people, and the reason we are still evolving today is because of the fears we have discovered as we develop in our daily interactions and efficiency. This behaviour is accepted by us as people subconsciously, and we do not seem to complain about it, as we are only exposed to and reliant on other people's predictions for our own world, due to our inability to understand it ourselves.

Fear can make itself continuously relevant to ignorance if ignorance refuses to interact with fear.

When we are able to listen to our minds, and pay attention to our own emotions and reactions to see the result for what it is rather than what others say it should be, based on their perspective, we become unpredictable, unstoppable and completely powerful. When we are able to see our fears within our own journey, and reflect on them thoroughly without defending any of our actions or reactions that seem unethical, we will change voluntarily and transform our lives through our own will.

Our fear needs our individual understanding, but when we don't give it what it needs, we allow our environment and the fears of other people in our environment to dominate and dictate to us through their own fears and needs, whilst they make their fear more important than ours and make us follow their direction.

Our environment and its people are strategic enough to be relative in their approach to making us think that our fear and interest is being looked after.

If we look carefully at consumerism as an example, although it is an economic theory that supports economic growth through a continuous increase in consumption of goods and services; consumerism in its entirety has become a problem for the world. Consumerism's continuous need for our fear, which exposes our unfulfilled and permanent needs and wants, allows it to manipulate us through strategies – such as made-to-break, trends, class markets, and other affordability and capability-decapitation strategies – in order to keep us buying.

Consumerism has caused our demand for goods and services to increase, making the need to produce those goods and services a priority; this has increased pollutant emissions, land use and deforestation, and accelerated climate change. It almost sound like our needs and wants are pressures for consumerism, but, in actual fact, our fears are being preyed upon. Today, the fear of relevance that comes from consumerism has resulted in rapid damage to our environments, our people's minds, our culture, our beliefs and our practices.

Fear is what makes the rich richer and the poor poorer.

Innate Fear

Incubating and Nurturing Fear

Innate fear, which is allegedly universal, is fear one has from birth. Innate fear serves the purpose of helping our survival by avoiding physical pain or death. Innate fear is apparently not taught, but is adopted naturally, like the fears of flying, heights, pitch darkness and scary dogs.

Fear is a perceived, inherent danger to our safety.

Whilst we may believe that innate fear is not taught, newborn babies, who have no real awareness of what fear is, and toddlers, whose nervous systems are immature, all cultivate their early stage of learning behaviour and expression of fear through their environment.

Environmental factors that may influence innate fear include parenting, culture, behaviour, status and beliefs. These factors also differentiate our experiences of fear, our reactions to fear and our growth process regarding fear.

As William Clement Stone said, “You are a product of your environment.”

Our fear is the fruit of our environment. The taste is conflicting.

The fear experiences of a newborn baby might not be formed until they reach the toddler stage when the child explores the environment themselves.

There are many different fears that a baby may develop. In addition to the fear of gravity, an infant could also develop mild cases of nyctophobia, scotophobia or lygophobia, which are the irrational fears of the night, the dark or darkness, respectively. Infants may also experience mild ochlophobia, which is an irrational fear or dislike of a crowd, especially of unfamiliar faces. They may also suffer from slight onomatophobia, which is an irrational fear or dislike of certain words, names, terms and objects, usually associated with traumatic experiences. They may also develop weak ligyrophobia, acousticophobia or phonophobia, all of which are names for the fear of sharp, loud, confusing or unidentified noises. Other fears that are very common with infants are mild cases of hydrophobia, which is an almost irrational fear of water, and the fear of feeling cold or the cold, which is called psychrophobia. Finally, some babies also find it difficult to stay in their own bed because of their slight clinophobia, which is the fear of going to or staying in bed or lying down. This can relate to a mild monophobia, which is the fear of being alone.

A toddler's experiences of fear may also be reduced or controlled through our parenting care and consideration of the possible hazards that may cultivate fear in the environment.

As with infants, there are several fears that toddlers may develop; the first of these is mild kainotophobia, which is an irrational fear of or resistance to change. They become familiar with certain environments and too clingy to accept any random changes. They may also develop a slight latrophobia, which is the fear of doctors due to possible untreated or unmanaged mild onomatophobia developed in infancy. Toddlers may also acquire a greater degree of hydrophobia due to it being untreated or unmanaged when it was only a mild or medium case. Although it is mainly dependent on the environment, some toddlers also develop a fear of dogs, which is called cynophobia. This is not only because of what a dog looks like but also because of the barking and irrational behaviour of dogs, which could also be connected to an untreated or unmanaged phonophobia. They may also have a persistent fear of being in bed due to being worried about nightmares, wetting the bed or being left alone.

We evolve through fear.

As we grow, learn and develop our own fears and factors in our own environment, we can choose to avoid, confront, ignore or learn to live with our innate fears. Our ability to climb, ride, fly, jump, drive, solve equations and problems, sleep alone, sleep in the dark, walk in the dark, be alone and cohabit with others are all signs of us understanding and dealing with our fears. These abilities also encourage us to believe that we can grow, we can see beyond our fear, and that our fear is only a feasible experience of an anticipated result.

When we are able to see or imagine the possible outcomes of an event, the possibilities we see make it real and not false. When our outcome isn't the one we desire, it shows that other results may also come from our fear. We need to open our minds to the other possible outcomes of an event or situation, rather than dwelling upon only the anxiety-inducing, damaging and not so encouraging presumptions.

It is fair to classify or define innate fear as an adaptive sense of safety and survival that can assimilate or identify what threatens our lives, directs or dictates our natural bodily responses, and suggests behavioural responses based on neural capacity, capabilities and cognition.

Fear Language

"Ouch" Moments

Besides the 10percent of the nervous system in our body that is set aside for our pain-control reflexes, there are diverse responses to pain. Our responses to pain are beyond natural neural reflexes (which are involuntary, almost instantaneous movements in response to a specific stimulus), but these responses depend on our cognition and are influenced by our growth environment.

The word "ouch", for example, is not in every language, but "ouch" sounds a more pleasant and acceptable response to an almost bearable pain than any other language. There are words in other languages and behaviours that are justifiable responses to an almost bearable pain, which could be perceived or judged as over-exaggerated response to a bearable pain by other people in other environments.

This is the same as for our innate fear, where our adaptive sense of safety and survival will assimilate and identify what threatens our life, and direct or dictate our natural bodily responses based on our cognition.

Our justifiable reaction when we are in fear, as influenced by our environment, is personal and should be respected and understood by those in other environments we may find ourselves in.

Regardless of how pleasant, unpleasant or over-exaggerated our reaction language and behaviour may be, it should never be a reason for us to be undermined.

Identity Fear

Desire

Identity fear, which allegedly also develops in us as we evolve, involves fear of judgement by others, public speaking, and verbal or vocal expression.

Our identity fear is driven by our known and unknown incompetence. Our unknown incompetence is driven by our anxiety and paranoia, whilst our known incompetence is our exposed weaknesses, secrets, guilt, or past or present mistakes.

Our unknown incompetence is sometimes confused with unknown outcomes, which is when we are fully aware of what our incompetence is but we are unable to accept the consequences of it. This happens when we think we are being attacked by others for being ourselves, but what is really happening to us is that we are unaware of what our shortcomings are and so don't see the problem with them, and we still don't want to be judged for them. We feel the sense of fear as paranoia at this stage, and we develop anxiety, especially because we can't predict what the outcome might be. These feelings happen at appraisals, disciplinary meetings, interventions, job interviews and feedback sessions.

We also sometimes confuse our known incompetence with known outcomes. This confusion happens when we fully understand the results of our shortcomings – such as embarrassment, rejection, failure, exposure, judgement and persecution, due to our pattern of experiences –and the consequences of them, but we still anxiously go ahead and face the expected result.

Our identity fears are more psychological than physical, and when we are careless in our approach, they may lead to lasting physical and psychological damage, such as death, mental illness, losses or injuries depending on our circumstances.

Our paranoia can ruin a lot of opportunities, relationships and interpersonal qualities when we allow it to linger. It may also be cultivated into unpleasant and unwanted behaviours that portray us as a potential problem in any environment we find ourselves in.

Identity fear can threaten our status in our communities, as we grow through our identity and our involvement in tribes and cultures, and we live together with others for companionship, reliance, alliances and legacy. Our survival may also be endangered through identity fear, as it can push us to become careless and irrational in our behaviour. Identity fear will beat us down to the point where we begin to comply with everything just for acceptance purposes. Finally, identity fear will squeeze us into self-sabotage through isolation, self-judgement, paranoia and anti-social behaviour traits.

Some of the aforementioned phobias are proof of these outcomes.

Other forms of identity fears relate to love and our connection with companionship and culture, in the fear of being alone, abandoned, disappointed, intimidated or rejected. Monophobia may also be explored further from this perspective to gain a greater understanding of our mindset when we are in fear.

Understanding that fear may hold us back from achieving or doing what is necessary is a good insight, and our ability to fully dissect our circumstances when possible gives us a clear and direct potential result for a certain action or reaction.

Our ability to act or react accordingly and productively may suppress our fear (or anxiety) and give us the courage to understand a process and see it through to achieve a desired result.

Template of Fear

Sub-consciousness

The actual template of our fear is irrational.

"**F**orget **e**verything **a**nd **r**un" and "**F**ace **e**verything **a**nd **r**ise" are mnemonics that can be used to categorise our fear. These perspectives are irrational as plans of possible action or reaction. They leave us no room for comprehension, but are simply a quick step-by-step guide or instruction regarding a first-hand feeling of fear.

Knowing that the purpose of most quotations regarding fear is to motivate or encourage us, it is clear that these mnemonics are pre-emptive decision that allows us to escape the actual feeling of fear. We might also decide to make that decision after feeling the emotions that come with our fear, depending on how relevant it is and what sort of action is required at that very moment contingent on the circumstances we are in.

Due to the emotions we attach to our fear, our fear naturally becomes an illogically logical emotion that we cannot help but feel.

The after-effect of our fear reaction is what we subconsciously classify and relate to as fear the most.

Having a feeling of doubt and being afraid of a stimulus are not mutually exclusive. Our feeling of doubt is a thought process that may or may not require any further action, whether that is rational or irrational. Although our feeling of doubt may sometimes be misunderstood as paranoia, our doubting mind and our paranoid mind are not mutually exclusive, and may not be interchangeable due to our intentions and behaviour. Being afraid, anxious or paranoid are totally different feelings that require certain actions or reactions to show physically or express our state of mind.

Forgetting everything and running could be logical, sensible and the quickest way of getting ourselves out of a dangerous situation, but this is also guided by our experiences that we have been told, have witnessed or encountered.

"**F**orget **e**verything **a**nd **r**un" as an encouraged reaction to fear is classified as flight mode, when considering the study of the amygdala.

Fear Is Inevitable

Mentality and exposure

"Safety is wise," or we should say, "safety is wisdom".

When we consider fleeing as a safety measure, we are also agreeing that fleeing is a reaction to the feeling of fear and not the fear itself. Safety is taught and, in some cases, learnt from experience as a chosen or anticipated reaction to stimuli. This is why it is a wise "decision".

To forget everything and run could also be perceived as cowardice by those in our environment. Depending on our personal experiences and our mindset, which other people in the environment may not understand, our fear of being judged, embarrassed, rejected or not being supported might not be relevant at the point we are experiencing our feelings, and will not be appropriate until we are totally safe or feel a sense of safety through our reflection and reassessment of our previous action or reaction to a stimulus.

We become powerful, unpredictable and free when we are able to understand that our feeling of fear is totally ours and that the feeling of being judged regarding our own safety by the people who are clearly self-centred in their opinion cannot make us feel any better. This does not make us arrogant or ignorant. Self-care is never self-centred. The ability to ask for help when needed must also be our sole decision in relation to our reflection and reassessment of our reaction and the outcome of our fear.

The dynamics of fear are too broad for anyone to be narrow-minded or naive about, and the idea of compartmentalising our experiences of fear by grouping and categorising them for diagnoses and treatment can sometimes be ignorant.

It is our diverse human mentality and exposure that puts our fear at numerous levels of experience as we evolve. Every person only has one fear system, and every single feeling of fear is tied to and stems from that one source: our brain. Our experiences, perspective, reactions and other major factors that determine our outcomes are what make the difference, even though our results may be similar or replicated at every level of growth. Our fear experiences are our growth experiences because, once we have experienced one level of fear, we become aware and may be better at reacting to it. We cannot conquer our fear; we can only react better to it through experience or growth.

Fear is an illogically logical emotion that we cannot help but feel. Our feeling of fear is inevitable, and there is nothing we can do to not feel fear. Our ability to manage fear accordingly and maybe effectively when possible could be the answer to a better life.

As mentioned previously, there is only one fear system in every single one of us, and this is naturally triggered by our amygdala. As described earlier in this book, the amygdala is a cluster of nuclei located in the temporal lobe of the brain, committed to detecting the emotional salience of stimulus. The amygdala is like a first-level processor which boots faster than any computer ever made. It is our instinctive and instantaneous human receiver and processor, which is highly involved in our emotional responses. Everything we do today regarding our growth, behaviour, motivation and lifestyle is tied to and will only function with the amygdala as the receptor.

Does this mean fear is life, or should we say life is fear?

If we answer yes, is fear transferable from person to person?

If we answer yes, can we conclude that fear is a cycle of feelings between people?

Our perception and the way we act or react when we are in fear is either subjective, objective, collective or mythical, depending on individual experiences, age, health, mentality, gender, belief, environment, etc.

Subjective Fear

In a sense, subjective fear is us exploring things, finding our own truths about things, and then building some sort of belief system, culture or pattern around our discovery or experience for achieving a desired result.

We are born with fear, we are all born different, and our experiences from birth also shape the beliefs around us, through our parents, families, friends and the aid we receive.

The stories of experiences of the fear, pain, sufferings of our parents or guardians and other personal or collective journeys built around our birth may also determine the names we are given by our parents or guardians and the name we may be called in our environment of growth. We may also choose to continue this name culture with our own children.

How we relate with our environment and how we grow are also controlled by the cultural patterns, interaction and activities surrounding us whilst we build our own personal perspective on our fear.

Objective Fear

Objective fears are tales or stories told to us about other people's experiences before our time, which are sometimes backed up with evidence or other similar stories we have heard from other people around the people around us.

Being told these stories can be a terrifying experience, as we build an image in our minds by listening to these experiences, and we replicate their experiences either through their facial expressions, tone of voice, gestures and behaviour throughout. We then buy into these experiences and make them ours, even when we don't experience what we are being told; our reactions then replicate those of the people who told us the story when we see any element of those experiences we were told about. Due to the memories, images and expressions we may have created psychologically, based on what we have been told, we may act or react accordingly as though we are living through other people's life experiences.

Objective fear could affect our skills, our health, our mentality, our interaction, our language and our expressions. Our tone of voice, our gestures and our lifestyle may also be impacted when we take on other people's experiences as ours. We imitate objective fear when we experience it. Our actions and reactions are not totally ours when we are experiencing it.

We become unlimited and free-spirited when we understanding that it is possible to change our perspective after the reaction to our fear experience.

How we reflect on and assess the outcomes of our experiences is highly imperative in our quest to do better.

Collective Fear

Collective fear relates mostly to our cultural, religious, social, ethnic, organisational, global and regulatory beliefs and practices.

In collective fear, our fears are more of the compliance type. When we feel like we may be prosecuted, shamed, isolated, embarrassed, undermined, rejected, ridiculed, intimidated or enslaved; therefore, we are compelled to comply for our safety and peace of mind.

These fears are taught or suggested. They are sometimes enforced and caused under influence, making us feel a voluntary sense of choosing to believe in, associate with or participate in these fears.

Collective fear is a kind of fear that may be damaging to our personal growth, mental health, survival and lifestyle too.

We may have to live by other people's opinions and standards, and deal only with foretold consequences. When we experience the consequences or results of collective fear, we are almost alone. The experience becomes a personal encounter, research or opinion. The encounter or opinion is never substantial enough for recognition by other people in that community unless we become influential, powerful or of a supposed good standing.

Collective fear is generational and can carry on through generations, unless we become or are seen as a misfit, a rebel or a rogue.

We bring about liberation when we are able to create a different kind of belief for a different kind of result through our behaviour, and construct an alternative practice to protect people from danger and unwanted outcomes. Beliefs and practices relating to collective fears are meant to be liberating not imprisoning.

Collective fear may boost our lives when, through it, we are able to manage to get the best result, and we may also benefit from it if we are able to push ourselves to the very top when we uphold or comply with its practices without violating them. Is this the way the world works?

Collective fear also creates unnecessary differences of opinion. It may cause more fear and harm than good for us because of its strong and extreme stance, which makes us consider certain environmental, social, educational, career and family choices for our own safety and peace of mind. We have explored this in the outcomes of some of the aforementioned phobias in this volume.

When we choose to remove or isolate ourselves from collective-fear beliefs and practices, then we may have to adopt others for our own safety and acceptance purposes. When we are unable to find alternatives, we become lonely, and we may feel a sense of neglect, weakness, etc. These outcomes are also explored in some of the aforementioned phobias in this chapter.

Sometimes, being comfortable in our own fear is better than adopting a collective one. We become peaceful within ourselves when we understand our own fear compared to when we follow other people's fears for relative comfort because of our phobia.

Mythical Fear

Mythical fear is mainly birthed through history books and the history we are told.

Mythical fear may be derived from our objective fear, but is mostly generated through our collective fear. Everyone knows about the fear, everyone believes in its impact and passes it on to others, but no one can really say they have technically experienced it. We cannot corroborate its true effects. It's a myth.

Mythical fear can be totally incapacitating, and the effect of it can prevent us achieving anything in life. We are constantly afraid of its consequences, so we try to not violate the made-up rules around it.

Our belief and desire to be immortal can be daunting and liberating at the same time; this is eliminating the fear of death and the fear of what might happen to us after death. Some of us wish to live forever, and we will do anything to achieve this, as long as death or loss of life is eliminated.

In other cases some of us might be willing to die in fear of continuing to exist or survival, and opt subconsciously for an alternative, better life after death, due to our overwhelming objective, subjective and collective fear pressures.

At times, our subjective experiences have already been influenced by our collective and objective perceptions. These interchangeable influences give us some beliefs and cultural practices, which suggest a lifestyle that is overwhelming enough to put our lives in more danger in the long run. We have no control over this as we are immature, unaware and psychologically vulnerable at this stage of our lives, and totally dependent on our environment for survival, growth, safety and provision.

On the flip side, we may also resist the collective and objective perceptions when we experience and re-experience events alone, and we become secretive about it for the personal pleasure, thrill or financial gain we get through the experience.

Fear has a way of making us imagine the impossible whether negative or positive. Our imagination when we are in fear depends on our personal, social, economic or other relative circumstances, and we might be able to find some other alternative result in our own interest.

Furthermore, we may not find any relevance to our feelings at all due to our understanding and our level of growth.

The Business of Fear

Accommodated feelings

The smell of fear is the fear sniffers' fix from their own fear.

Fear sniffers are people who exploit our fears for their own personal gain. They are able to smell our fear because of the vulnerabilities in our reactions. The ability to manipulate other people's fear is a skill that gives the exploiters some relevance. This is because they are also afraid, just like we are, and the solution to their own fear is our vulnerability.

Fear sniffers' skills allow them to lead and control us when we are in fear. Our fear gives them confidence. Our behaviour when we are in fear gives them the platform to brainwash and manipulate us in order exploit our beliefs and vulnerabilities for their own gain.

Fear is a commodity that only you can sell and pay for at the same time; that is, until you're bold enough to make that fear totally intangible to the fear sniffers. When we are able to handle our fear and manage our interactions even when we are in fear; that is when we make our fear an intangible commodity for the exploiters.

We are also able to use and display our inner strength when we are in fear. This makes us invincible to fear seekers and sniffers.

Fear is valuable to those who can find and suggest it, by selling the idea of it and marketing it to larger groups and early adopters for personal gain.

We seek to buy solutions when we are afraid. The process of seeking for answers requires listening to and bargaining with the symptoms of our fear, and that adds more to what we started with.

In the end, we accumulate multiple fears and our one solution becomes several. We end up solving none of these fears, but instead we become victims and guinea pigs for multiple tests and diagnostics for fear.

Why do we want to adopt the ideas of fear seekers and sniffers when we can seek and find our own ideas ourselves?

Fear will make a negative process look positive, due to its justifiable interests.

Our fear is naturally logical, which is positive, but our reaction process is illogical most of the time, and that is negative. When we are in fear, we can justify our reactions, which are mostly negative, because of our perspective and our anticipated result.

When we are able to see beyond our fear at appropriate times, our results can transform us and our environment, reducing the cycle of fear.

Fear sees opportunities in a crisis rather than priorities, and might take measures to sustain and maintain its interests. A crisis is identified as such mostly because of people's reactions rather than the actual problem. Fear sniffers and seekers are extremely good at finding the opportunities in a crisis, and their opportunities lie within our fear reactions.

In a crisis, opportunists prioritise their own interests, and focus on how to sustain and maintain the crisis in a way that is subtle enough to make the crisis appear solved, but where it has been embedded to protect their own interest.

We are strong when we understand our crisis, and have developed the ability to not react but rather to respond accordingly to solve the crisis. The ability to neutralise and not magnify a crisis through our reactions will bring good to us and our environment.

Fear is an advertisement of vulnerability to sniffers and once they have sniffed it, some people are ready to cash in on it.

The most intriguing part of our lives is that we voluntarily believe our fear is a major problem and a hindrance to us making our goals attainable. Yes, we may be right about it being overwhelming enough to consume our lives, but this is again down to us reacting rather than responding. Once we believe that our fear is a major problem in our lives, we have found a buyer, who is us. We are also the ones who will be motivated to pay for our fear to go away. Ka-ching! This is the sound of the cash register in our shop, and we are not the people cashing in on our fear. The ones we have advertised our fear to are the ones cashing in. These are the ones who think they are smart enough to manipulate us into believing that we have a big problem on our hands and make us believe they can help us take it away by making us follow their lead at a cost that we also have to pay. We can take our fear back and get a refund through understanding.

Fear's major unique selling point is self-belief. Once you believe it, you are trapped. How messed up and twisted is that?

It is quite fascinating that we can sell a commodity and be the one to also buy it, and still make a loss in the end. Our fear – sold, bought and paid for by us– is not a gain for us but a loss in many ways.

Fear is a *victim* who expresses feelings of fear and reacts by calling the attention of the *hero*, who seems to know the way and is the *one* who can solve the problem of fear and save the day with the skills developed and influenced by the *enabler*, who motivates and brings out the confidence, boldness and courage in *others* waiting to express their fear.

Fear is a cycle of evolving feelings accommodated by life for survival, safety and relevance. Survival, safety and relevance are valuable to our fear, but whichever one gets our attention determines our intention, either good or bad, and that intention will lead us to our outcomes, either good or not so bad.

The language, culture, interaction and path of our fear are understood by sniffers. These languages, cultures, interactions and paths are value based and cannot be stopped due to their functionality (safety, survival and relevance).

We must function and function well, even in our fear.

Fear may continue to pay for its values until there is some understanding of a solution and management through growth. When we are able to understand ourselves, our fear becomes a part of our growth.

The solution to our issues becomes a process for us, and managing the challenges that come with our fear becomes the true value of our lives. Our sustainable fear will move away from being a psychological growing pain and towards becoming a sustainable development value.

These values are known to be respect for nature, including ourselves; individual and shared responsibility; solidarity; equality; tolerance; and freedom.

The Pleasurable Fear

Fear classified

Our fear is sometimes a feeling we may wish not to disclose to others due to loyalty, the thrill of it or indulgence, and not just for the other aforementioned factors. The idea of secrets, thrills and indulgence also fits with our fear and may also fit with our need for companionship and association simply for thrills and participation purposes.

Some of our subjective-fear experiences can build some sort of craving, thrill, fixation or indulgence, which we may not necessarily want to share, fix or be saved from. We sometimes want to thrive, bask and live in our fear just because it is pleasurable. This sort of fear in us may extend to other experiences, but it is never the same.

There could be many of us in one room, who all have the same fear stimuli, but the perspective, sensation and reaction we each give and gain from same feeling is diverse. Our diverse perspectives, sensations and reactions also diversify our outcomes.

Our journey or our mind travel through this sort of fear experience releases certain toxins, which create a sensation in our body, and once we experience the thrill, we may become a thrill junkie over time, and the secret indulgence of this fear becomes our go to when we need to feel that sensation, whilst we subconsciously build our brain memory and space for that experience.

Some of our experiences are built through abuse or violation, and these experiences may have been very traumatic at first, but in some cases were not enough to kill or relatively destroy anything or anyone and sadly, in other cases, may have caused mental illness, disabilities and death.

The outcome of some of our fear experiences might be shameful, embarrassing or demeaning from other people's perspectives, but not to us.

This is why some of our fear experiences can be classified in different ways. The type of fear being described here may be classified or defined as a post-traumatic pleasurable thrill, which may have been caused by a traumatic experience. This feeling may not have been life threatening, but it is damaging enough to trigger the production of pleasure and thrill toxins, rather than stress, pain or distress. This could be seen medically and concluded to be a disorder.

A psychological fixation could be classified as an example of a post-traumatic pleasurable thrill. This may also be found in obsessive compulsive disorder or in a psychosexual disorder. By definition, a fixation is a distinct and persistent psychological focus on the pleasure-seeking sensation experienced at an earlier stage of development. A fixation occurs when an issue, conflict or disruption happens to us in our early development stage, which alters our growth process.

Such an unresolved, altering, development-stage experience could be classed as a traumatic experience that leaves us stuck and focused on that experience, and thus unable to move past it or develop psychologically beyond the experience.

These experiences create a memory and sensation that we may develop into pleasure or fantasy, and then form into a practice and a lifestyle throughout our growth process.

Thrilling Fear

Marvel

A traumatic thrill from fear is simply where fear meets pleasure.

This is not PTSD and it has no relevance to this type of fear in any way, as it may not be diagnosed as a sickness. If it does get diagnosed as a sickness, then some of the thrills that we have available today, through experiences – such as amusement and theme parks, and those themed events designed to cater for certain groups of people – may be invalid and totally ineffective. Some of our human-evolution-related discoveries regarding personality and human growth will be invalid if we diagnose every condition and result of human-survival experiences as a sickness. Our fear is not a sickness, nor is it a deficiency.

Traumatic thrills are totally personal, and our reactions and outcomes may be different due to environment, gender, age, exposure and the circumstances surrounding the initial traumatic experience.

We have the tendency to be totally protective over our fear to make it totally exclusive, classified and justifiable. By listing all these fear experiences and the reactions we might have, it becomes clear that we are powerful when we are in fear, we are vulnerable when we are in fear, we are predictable when we are in fear, but we are also unpredictable when we are in fear.

It's like we become a Marvel character when we are in fear, showing all kinds of impossible skills, performing stunts, opening our minds to other possible intelligences, exploring extremely quickly using a learnt pattern of action, or demonstrating a new and impossible reaction to something we have never seen before.

Seeing all the Marvel movies actually provides a good representation of what fear could become in a very short space of time.

Our level of sensation and feeling that triggers certain behaviours, character, superpowers and strengths allows us to discover more about who and what we are, and how we can also be when we are in fear.

Fear makes us human.

Sometimes, our fear allows us to function effectively. At other times, our fear allows us to think of ways to survive, ways to grow, ways to be safe, ways to be healthy, ways to be secure, ways to stay ahead, ways to be relevant, ways to generate wealth, ways to be successful, ways to be immortal and ways to create a life after death.

Fear for Purpose

The interest

Fear is a natural human neurological activity that occurs for a purpose. From this it can be concluded that fear is created.

Our fear gives us the ability to generate insight into our needs, and our needs allow us to see opportunities and solutions. However, the solutions we see may be solely individualistic or general. This is a purpose, and purpose in this context means reason.

Our human functionalities justify our fear, and, without fear, there will be no need for growth or evolution. Our fear makes us want to be better than we used to be.

The meaning of purpose in the context of our fear is respect, compliance, obedience, followership, agreement, slavery, labour, love, allowance, allegiance, responsibility and loyalty. We are able to achieve all these because we want to make sure everything works well for our personal or collective purpose.

Anything that stops our effort to achieve functionality is seen as dysfunctional, and removing these dysfunctions is valid enough for our purpose.

Some of our reaction to our purpose in life may have side effects or other unpleasant results, and this is where understanding comes in.

We should be able to trace back our steps if need be, for restitution when necessary, to repair damage, and to clear away some of the footsteps or footprints we had made to allow for new ones to achieve our desired result.

We have created so much fear in ourselves today, and this is why we are still in debt, war, competition and committing atrocities.

Our fear reactions make us create regulations that are ineffective but functional, whilst we hope to revisit them for future development to meet future needs. These are unsustainable solutions. Our fear also pushes us design policies that seem effective but are not functional, whilst we aspire to serve a purpose, but we have only generated funds for ourselves and created more fear for the general public whom we are meant to be serving.

We must understand that, in our functioning world of fear, nobody is bad; we are all just afraid.

Nobody means to harm others, but, in order to protect their own interests, they might need to compromise on other people's safety. Nobody means to hurt others, but, to have enough for themselves and their own generation, they feel the need to and the sense in making other people pay. Nobody wants to intimidate others, but, in order to be relevant and stay at the top, someone will need to do the work. Nobody wants to destroy anyone's business or livelihood, but sustainability and immortality have become necessities.

Our fear is a realm. This is a realm where we are in our own mind and mildly self-centred in some cases, as we create solution for our environment and others who may not necessarily need our help, not because they do not need help, but the help needed requires a different perspective to the one we anticipate they might need.

Our realm of fear is a sense, a place or a domain of possible capabilities for relative purposes. This means that we can reform fear and gain some sort of positive result from it if we choose to.

There are a few functioning systems that we have created and value today that are only effective due to the fear we have inflicted through them.

The Culture of Fear

The encounter

Developing a culture is one of the most effective ways of creating value in people today. It functions mainly through the mutual and collective ideas, customs, intelligence and social behaviour of a particular group of people.

A culture creates a platform for the purpose of social representation through meaning, tradition, security and legacy. Culture creates a lifestyle – or a way of life, if you prefer – for identity purposes, and also to give us some sense of belonging, belief and something to hold on to throughout our lives. Culture creates tradition through elements such as language, music, arts, history, cuisine, tribe, interaction, clothing and accessories, and religion (in some cases) as part of the tradition for effective functionality in order to nurture and develop ourselves from within.

The idea behind culture is to help raise the community or society through mutual interest, and when everyone in this nurtured culture believes and behaves accordingly, growth is easier, and protecting cultural values is also better.

Our objective fear may be influenced through culture. Our culture sets the tone in our environment and so everything in our environment suggests a certain way of life that only offers us one set of doctrines and traditions to be practised for a collective outcome.

Our diverse cultural beliefs can sometimes be narrow-minded and wilfully ignorant in an effort to protect us and force us through fear into only believing what our traditional values have to offer, implying that anything outside of this will be wrong, opposite or invaluable, and may lead us to destruction, alienation, extradition, prosecution or death.

Culture is represented through our family, race, town, tribe or, in a bigger form, country, and it provides values in which everything and everyone is focused on nurturing, protecting, mentoring, and influencing language and behaviour through oneness, togetherness and unity.

Our diverse family traditions and culture are very strong, and provide a foundation that allows for punishment, isolation, unrewarded efforts, abuse, disowning and possible death if and when we violate, disobey or do not comply with the family traditions.

As valuable as our culture is, it can inflict so much fear in us to the point where we lose our identity and become aimless throughout our lives. Sometimes, when we don't comply with our culture, our set doctrine inflicts fear in us and puts us in danger, making us vulnerable, in the hope that we might come to our senses in the end.

Our fear keeps us in check, limits or stops us from seeing things from other non-relative perspectives.

A culture is a value-based movement that sometimes creates invaluable differences where there shouldn't be any. Our cultural doctrine and practices can create anti-social behaviour and hostility in our social and multicultural environments, and, unless we educate ourselves about other existing cultures and respect their doctrines, we may lose our identity and, eventually, lose our lives.

We create chaos when we are unable to see a culture for what it should be, and we must be open-minded enough not to change our identity due to pressure, but to be strong in understanding and empathetic enough to let others express themselves without us being affected or offended by it. Our inability to accept and respect diverse expressions of cultural practices without opposing or inflicting our own cultural consequences upon others is also a subconscious reaction to our own fear. This may also create a bigger threat to our diversified environment.

These results and outcomes are also seen in some of the phobias explored in this volume.

Our cultural beliefs may also create long-standing fears of extinction, economic downturn, slavery, etc., which makes our cultural practices totally xenophobic. Whilst we act upon instincts and the reactions dictated by our culture – which could lead to discrimination, prejudice and supremacy – this makes our culture and cultural beliefs dominate all others.

Some of our cultural responsibilities have also been extended into social responsibilities, where certain social and ethical behaviours become acceptable and good practice. When we choose not to comply with some of the cultural practices imposed in our chosen environment, we are judged for our social irresponsibility and sometimes deemed to have some behavioural issues that suggest a psychological deficiency.

Culture is value related, and its values only dwell in people who wholeheartedly decide to live by its doctrines. Real culture also shows respect for other existing cultures whilst it enjoys what is brought into an environment of coexisting cultures.

Our cultural values shouldn't inflict fear in us but should liberate us by empowering us to be comfortable in our own skin, whilst we appreciate and respect other cultural beliefs in our daily encounters and interactions. When we live in cultural fear, we are limited to our cultural provisions, and everything else outside of this is seen to be abominable.

We have unlimited access to unrestricted cultural resources when we are able to understand other cultural practices around us, whilst we value our own, and we will be able to enjoy the values of a multicultural environment.

Fear Pressure

The sense of belonging

Hierarchical Culture

This hierarchical culture is about control, structure, stability and efficiency through leadership, laws, beliefs and traditions. It is somewhat selfish and emotional, because it's based on oppressive leadership and imposed efficiency.

Hierarchical culture is just like a family type of culture, but more in the context of a corporate environment where we are ranked according to our quality, qualification and importance.

In hierarchical culture, some of the outcomes of the fears in other people in our environment may already be influencing the growth of those in our environment by making people around us have certain behavioural traits.

The phobias that dominate growth in our environment, including our reactions to them and the ensuing results, are the factors that may have shaped the culture in our environment.

A hierarchical cultural environment can be encouraging at times and in other times motivational. However, it can also be judgemental and damaging to our self-esteem if we have experienced a misunderstanding, a non-empathetic dismissal or a demotion when we are not able to meet the cultural standards set for performance.

Our fear at this level of pressure could make us lose our self-worth and other qualities that makes us unique, all through the process of meeting demands and being productive with a total commitment to the betterment of the environmental and cultural practices.

Our set targets and other key values are designed to qualify us to take part in the environmental practices, and once this is lacking, we become a figure of concern with respect to the organisation's progress.

Our sense of belonging and confidence in this cultural environment should allow us to interact well in other environments when our association and affiliation with our existing environment is our ticket and access to other environments where our skills may be considered helpful.

Whom we know, where we work, what we do, how we work, with whom we work and how much we earn makes us relevant at home with our parents, with our friends and acquaintances, and in other social and political environments we might be involved in.

This is where quotations such as "Show me your friends, and I will tell you who you are", "Birds of a feather flock together", "What surrounds us is what's within us",

"Winners have no interest or association in the opinions, actions and affairs of losers", "If you agree to work with uninspiring fossils, it's only a matter of time before you will become one", and "Bad company corrupts good character" (1 Corinthians 15:33) are all used to make us feel inferior, or superior for that matter. These quotations inflict fear and anxiety strategically in some of us, and once the seed is sown, some people may end up being unfulfilled for the rest of their lives.

Just as our fears are transferable from generation to generation, our fears are also transferable from one environment to the other. Hierarchical culture creates a transferable fear.

We carry our fear in our minds, and so we become our fear. The fear we become shows through our behaviour and language, exposing us to judgemental people or environments. We also become judgemental due to the character we have cultivated. Hierarchical culture consumes our character, just like a religion, where our natural and instinctive reaction to our environment is arrogant and defensive. When we allow the fear to consume us, we become timid, insecure and unstable.

Adhocracy Culture

Adhocracy culture is another corporate cultural practice that relates to dynamics, entrepreneurship, innovation, risk-taking and doing things first. It's about getting things first, leading things and totally monopolising things.

Adhocracy culture requires being consistently flexible to change, leading the change, taking the initiative, taking risks and making it work.

When we are in an adhocracy culture, we become the elite: the one percent of the one percent. Intelligence, wealth, people and possessions are the major values of adhocracy.

We are constantly trying to prove a point and doing as much as possible not to lose face in our association with adhocracy. The fears of losing dignity and identity are important fear factors in an adhocracy culture.

The journey to the top is as hard as the fall from that very top.

The idea of being relevant through an adhocracy culture can motivate us to educate ourselves and learn new skills in order to fit into the culture. Adhocracy requires certain character traits and behaviours that show status naturally.

The fear of judgement is the major issue in an adhocracy mindset. The fear generated in an adhocracy culture actually makes us calm, cool and collected. We display a character that is almost inhuman or superhuman. However, our fear in an adhocracy culture can make us paranoid and push us into isolation.

An adhocracy culture can create moral distancing, where we become disengaged from people, our environment and practices, even though we are seen as a role model. However, an adhocracy culture should liberate us to engage with our journey, appreciate processes, have empathy and be emotionally intelligent.

Our character in an adhocracy culture is dismissive, apprehensive and sometimes immoral, as we believe we are above the law, and our downfall will be the downfall of everything and everyone around us. We live by our sense of entitlement, and we become self-centred.

Our fear reaction in an adhocracy culture must affect everything and everyone, and when it doesn't, we throw tantrums. This fear also humbles us, but in a self-seeking way, rather than through the self-evaluation of our reactions to achieve a better result. When we feel humiliated as a result of this fear, it causes us to maltreat people and things in our environment when we should be more careful and considerate, especially when we know that our behaviour influences our environment. Our sense of superiority and leadership should help us connect with our environment, be free to express our fear in a precise and personal way, and lead with respect to understanding growth.

Our ability to understand the difference between the subjective fear we are afflicted with and other objective and collective fears helps us to manage our personal challenges without making our fears epidemic or pandemic for our own gain.

Social and Material-Based Culture

A social and material-based culture is results oriented with a massive focus on competition, achievements, possessions, dignity and legacy. Our behaviour in a social and material-based culture may be influenced by the adhocracy culture.

A social and material-based culture is broad and more influential than most of the other existing cultures, as it controls our survival, social interactions and acceptance. This type of culture affects all other cultures, because all our other cultural values are tested and controlled by it. Our family name, our religion, our family possessions, assets, pedigree, affluence, etc. are all compared with others to determine our social position and relevance.

Our level of fear in a social and material-based culture can push us into a lot more than we can handle, and if we are irrational in our reactions, we might not fit in anywhere due to the pressure, expectations and requirements we set for ourselves.

Our fear is shown in our sense of neglect, isolation, identity loss, loneliness and acceptance, and perhaps through an inferiority complex. We expend a lot of effort to accumulate social media likes, followership, compliments and recognition. We become competitive in our approach to everything. We become hypocritical, but think we are being diplomatic. We lose all sense of respect, just so that our goals are attainable.

Our fear in social and material culture makes us bite off more than we can chew. We put our lives in danger, whilst we think we are following success principles to achieve our goals. We lose our moral compass when we are in fear, as our ability to judge what is right and what is wrong is lost in our quest for social acceptance. We allow our environment to direct and decide on our actions and reactions.

Fear stands and falls for everything

Our fear in a social and material-based culture makes us frail and unstable. When we are afraid in this type of culture, we have no value or self-worth, as every social and material value becomes our value subconsciously. Individualism is one of the values within a social and material-based culture.

Our expression when we are in fear is only admirable when we are able to share our principles rather than being controlled by our social and materialistic environment.

When we are in fear, our individualistic culture gives us the ability to focus on our strengths, whilst we enjoy the benefits of our social group and culture. This individualistic culture also motivates others around us to value themselves more whilst they also enjoy the interrelationship. Our fear in a social and material-based culture should encourage us to build an interpersonal culture with empathy.

Everything Culture

Diversity

The fears that exist throughout our generation may reoccur in our cultural behaviour, and history has a way of repeating itself, and that is only through culture.

Culture can create a lasting fear in us.

We thrive when we see culture for what it is, learn from it and understand the history. If we are open-minded and respectful towards other existing cultural beliefs and practices, we will have access to explore new things if we choose to. We are also able to position ourselves for greater opportunities, and gain insight into ways of having a thorough understanding of and empathy for others, allowing them to express themselves without being affected or offended.

Our ability to make constructive conclusions beyond our cultural beliefs is coherent when we understand the context, processes, practices, mentality, environment and circumstances of fear that are totally different from ours. When we understand other cultural fears, we will see that –even when our fears, experiences and results may be similar –they are contextually different.

Melting Pot

The Three Wise Cultural Men

The fear and cultural experiences of a *man who lives in a jungle* are different from both the *man who lives in a wildlife park* and the *man who lives in the city*.

Putting together the jungle and the wildlife-park life experiences in a city life experience and environment, where animal-rights laws are enforced and observed, will cause chaos.

The man from the jungle, who is a *hunter*, might see animals as *livestock* and run towards the animals, hoping to be lucky and make a kill.

The man from the wildlife park might see the scene, and feel the need to run and protect the man from the jungle from danger, either by capturing the animals and preventing them from reaching the man from the jungle, or by creating a safe space or haven for that man.

In his natural habitat, the man from the city could see the man from the wildlife park running after the man from the jungle, who is trying to get lucky and kill livestock, and the man from the city may assume that both other men are illiterate and know nothing about animal rights, and so he may also run, but only to protect the animal from both men. The man from the city might also label both the hunter and the park ranger as *dangers to his environment*, and may take matters into his own hands with the aim of protecting the animals.

The people in the city's *neutral* or *liberal* cultural environment could also deem all three men to be criminals and apprehend them for public safety.

This is pure cultural misunderstanding by all men and the people in the city, and the only victim here is the animal, which would not be able to defend itself in the city's court of law. However, the man from the jungle, the man from the wildlife park and the law-abiding citizen from the city would be able to make their cases in court to justify their actions in mutually beneficial legislation for multicultural environment.

We certainly notice the contextual changes in their personality traits from all perspectives.

It is imperative that we all work together to achieve a compromise for coexistence in comfort for all, without anyone feeling left out or alienated in a developing world with diverse life experiences.

Our cultural fears should not separate us; they should instead bring us together comfortably, so that we are all fulfilled in our subjective, objective and collective goals, even in our separate environments. Our cultural fears must liberate us to express ourselves in a non-judgemental environment without needing to offend or defend ourselves, but so that we are understood to the point where we also begin to learn and benefit from other cultural and environmental values.

Religious Fear

Nature

A religion is a theological system of beliefs and practices attached to certain moral and ethical values, that is totally devoted to worshipping a supernatural power, which is often one or more personal gods and goddesses.

The study of history, doctrines and teachings of religious laws reveal that these religions promise a better life through compliance, leadership, mentoring of other humans, developing environments and in some cases, converting other people to follow the same path.

A religion may also be classified as a philosophical tradition or lifestyle, which studies fundamental principles that improve attitudes, human behaviour, and its environment to create a more purposeful and well preserved environment.

Religion combines nature, its reactions, resources, history, people and mythologies to determine behaviours and culture that may result in some good and that represent one or more deities worthy of worship.

It is believed that religion is part of culture, and has been the root of and led culture in the Western tradition, but when we understanding that religion is beyond the Western tradition, we will see that religion is built subconsciously, with cultural experiences and values in mind. Culture in itself is also built through nature, its reaction, history and the behaviour of the people in a geographical location. This means that the behaviour of the people in a chosen location is determined by their environment, and if the environment allows for certain mythologies, it will then be easy for the people to create their own method of control for themselves and their environment.

Natural disasters, seasons and resources are major determinants of our life experiences, and these experiences mould our behaviour in our chosen geographical location. The behaviour moulded based on the factors associated with our environment is formed through our reactions. Our reactions, which are revealed through our behaviour, will eventually cultivate our chosen way of life, and that is religion. This has led to the saying "religion is a way of life".

Our cultivated way of life, which we call religion, is demonstrated and defined through our character, and our character is our mental and moral qualities that are distinctive to each and every one of us. Religion then becomes our individual mental and moral qualities that enhance our chosen way of life.

Origin of Religious Fear

Way of life

By definition, mythology is the study and interpretation of often sacred tales or fables of a culture known as myths (Joshua J. Mark, 2018).

These myths are in the folklore genre, and consist of narratives or stories that play a fundamental role in a society, such as founding tales, and the main characters in myths are usually gods or goddesses, demigods, or supernatural humans.

In this context – knowing that geographical location is a big factor in our diverse cultures and that religion naturally combines nature, its reactions and resources to provide some history and tales for its people to develop a culture from –we can understand that myths are created and built through people's perspectives on nature, its interaction and its reactions. We can also understand that culture is part of religion and not the other way around.

The god of iron in Haitian Voodoo and Yoruba mythology is Ogun. He is a loa (Haitian god in the voodoo cult), an orisha (Southern Nigeria, South America and the

Caribbean name for gods, goddesses and demigods), a warrior, a powerful spirit of metal, and also the spirit of rum and rum making. He presides over fire, iron and hunting. He was clearly seen to be a spirit because of his skills and the wonders he could perform through his interaction with natural resources, such as metal; maybe he was seen as a spirit man who could make impossible things possible because of how he could control the form of iron and sparks of fire through various methods.

Without diving too far into the history of this god of iron, we can recognise that this power was discovered by a person in a certain location who then shared this experience with his community and was recognised for his great supernatural powers. The community would later create a shrine to worship Ogun after his death, and, as a result, he would be remembered as Ogun the spirit man who provided protection and methods by which a result is achieved for his community. It would also become a belief that, by building shrines and altars for Ogun, the worshippers could gain Ogun's spiritual favour to acquire methods by which a result is achieved.

The god Ogun clearly isn't Western, and he is still currently being worshipped and revered by his followers for methods by which a result is achieved. This is an example of a mythical fear, which was mainly birthed through oral history and may have been derived from a subjective-fear experience but was mostly generated and built through collective fear.

Everyone in the Ogun-worshipping region knows of this fear, they all believe in that fear, and some may also say that they have experienced the wonders of the god of iron. Their experiences have created a reaction, controlled behaviour and built a mythological belief system that later turned to a culture that is considerable enough to be a part of their religion or their way of life.

Today, the image of Ogun is carved into a shrine, so he may be worshipped as a spirit who can provide methods by which a result is achieved, and a way of life has been built around it. Just to clarify, when we show reverence, we may feel a sense of deeper respect as a meaning. The actual physical ritualistic image we build around our belief to show honour and respect for that belief is called a shrine. In some cases, the practice of offering worship to the physical shrine that was built as a continuous expression of reverence and adoration is what started a religion.

Apart from the physical image, the image of the shrine is also imprinted in the worshippers' minds, and so, wherever they find themselves, they are able to worship their god and connect with the shrine in their subconscious mind without the physical shrine to bow to.

The fear inflicted through religion isn't meant to be of the frightening type, but much more of gentle approach in confidence. In religion, it is widely known that fear is inflicted as a way to teach, lead and control a people in order to influence their way of life. This influence on a way of life is shown through mental strength, capabilities, displays of supernatural powers, influence, affluence and intelligence, which are all reflective of the god they worship, so that others can believe in and follow this same god.

Imposing Fear

Beggar's choice

Poverty is a simple analogy of the condition of fear that could be reflected through the idiom "a beggar has no choice". Poverty and a lack of resources are factors used for control in addition to other strategic ways of conditioning people to comply with religious doctrines. Poverty doesn't allow for choice.

A poverty mindset can lead us into a religion in which a better life is promised. Our fear of the unknown may give us anxiety at times, and, in every religion, anxiety is seen as a bad spiritual or mental affliction that needs some spiritual or psychological attention. The attention needed is either from the gods, who have supernatural powers to cure the affliction; from the rich, who have enough money to enslave; from the elite, who have all the wealth through their intelligence and are ready to direct us in their own quest to find fulfilment; or from the psychologists, who may also be seen as supernatural people with answers to transform poverty into wealth if we are able to follow certain strategic steps that have been put together as a general rule to cure all kinds of poverty.

The fear of lasting poverty and the mentality it causes in people, which leads to anxiety, needs a cure. Furthermore, the people in poverty will definitely do anything proposed to get out of their situation. This willingness by the poor to do what is necessary gives the influencers the power of opinion to diagnose problems and create solution with respect to their self-proclaimed ability to change people's lives, and so influencers will take advantage of the circumstances and create some pattern, steps or doctrine for others to follow. If and when these steps are not followed, it can be said that the follower has failed in the process of transformation and may need to start again or instead follow alternative processes drafted by the influencer.

This suggests that the subjects' greater level of fear of failure and self-sabotage are exposed to the influencers, and that gives the influencers total control of the subjects' lives until such time as the subjects are able to complete the process in order to have a sense of accomplishment. The subjects' accomplishments may create a new doctrine for the followers, through the observed personal experience, encounter and results from their training process.

If we look at the world today, we will see and hear testimonials relating to quite a number of practices and doctrines in religions that are run by the same circle of people who claim to have gone through the same process in the same environment as their followers, whilst they are developing themselves to become leaders and influencers.

These aspiring influencers tend to come up with new practices that criticise other practices that exist for their doctrines, and create scaremongering strategies, and then they place greater value on their own practice by promising to liberate people through their own alternative and better approach to those practices.

Religion has evolved as quickly as people have. It has kept the control system effective enough, regardless of people's growth, exposure and understanding.

Worshippers and followers will always continuously revere the supernatural and the advanced system that has been created, which may be due to the level of fear inflicted in them.

Religion is meant to enhance people's growth in understanding, and give people moral, mental and social strengths to help them navigate through the journey of life. Religion was also built to direct people towards the resources needed for life in order to create sustainable life for the generation to come. Religion in context is meant to enhance individuals' spiritual and mental connections to their unique capabilities in order to create more potential in regard to creating solutions to social, economic and environmental issues.

Our fear from religion has shielded us from the morals that liberate us from being vulnerable and frail, and has eroded our social, spiritual and mental interpersonal-interaction skills for control purposes.

Our fear from religion limits our achievements, and blocks us from accessing and understanding our full unique potential.

Our fear from religion has enslaved us into believing we cannot achieve anything unless we submit our future to be directed by others who are also limited by their culture and exposure.

Our fear from religion dehumanises our unique growth experiences and suggests that the practices guided by its culture and environment are the only path to fulfilment.

Our fear from religion stops us from expressing our true experiences of life due to our fear of judgement and rejection.

Our fear from religion, which is meant to make us a growing part of its culture, has made us rebellious due to it having a monopoly on that culture.

Our fear from religion has influenced us to become judgemental, arrogant and narrow-minded in our ways, as we condemn other religious practices and cause divisions in the environment we are responsible for.

Our fear from religion has kept us emotionally dependent and lazy enough to not push for results, whilst it reminds us that if we remain under its control, our needs will be taken care of without us lifting a finger.

When we are afraid, we become resentful and that resentment may lead us into other reactions that are deemed unacceptable in our religious environment. Those reactions can alienate us from our religious communities, leaving us with no sense of identity or belonging. This is why our resentment sometimes pushes us to revolt and seek alternative ways of life in order for us to express our feelings.

Fear of Revolution

Expression

An uprising against a religion is a rebellious movement that criticises, refuses or revolts against the orders, laws, oppressive powers and influence of religious practices. The criticism of such an uprising is due to the limited knowledge, inadequacies, inconsistencies and hypocrisies of existing religious practices.

This group of people who are rebelling do not agree with the idea of being controlled by an entity and believe in a life with freedom of thought. This group of people may be seen as afraid of being controlled or not being knowledgeable enough to understand some human ethical principles, but they have actually studied the inadequacies in the religious practices throughout history and have ascertained inconsistencies in those practices. Their ability to look at the religious leadership system and find a hypocritical stance or alternative outcomes with no evidence of the existence of any supernatural powers or any plausible facts to back up the beliefs has given them a reason to question the authenticity of religious practices.

The uprisers are wary of the mythological systems of control that may lead people astray. They may be scholars, or highly intelligent and logical thinkers who are unable to experience what other people may have experienced to validate their opinions and beliefs.

Fear will create a life for its beliefs, and it will continue to align itself with the life it has created to justify itself.

For the purposes of awareness, opposition and sometimes relevance, uprisers may end up expressing their opinion in disbelief, and in doing so will need to convince people with their own theories, research, findings and experience in order to convert or redeem people from their supposed concurrent spell for a more sustainable lifestyle.

The process of doing so creates disbelief and a new belief system, which will need another pattern and another way of life. The alternative way of life also will build a new culture, whether it turns into a full-blown religion or not, and it must become another movement with a lifestyle. That in itself is a religious practice and another denomination of fear.

Fear of revolution may also be classified as fear coming from a rebellious group of believers who may have reacted to the teachings, doctrines and traditions of a religious practice, and have exposed and weakened the belief in those practices, due to their fear of consequences and persecution that would occur as a result of their inability to comply with the religious rules.

This group of people believe in the supernatural, unlike the ones that criticise, refuse and revolt against it, but they will only practise the elements of the religion that soothe their personality, gender, circumstances, location and way of life. This can only happen through subjective experiences of fear, which may have created different encounters and results compared to the rules laid out by their former practice and their presumed results, which are now contrary to what they have seen or felt.

These types of people pick and choose what parts of the religion work for them and everything else is paid no attention. They are the sort of people who will also build a persona around religion, will see religion only from their own point of view, and will profess these opinions until people are converted and become like them.

Fear is creative and very good at criticism. Fear can oppose very strongly and revolt rigorously. Fear will build a whole new life before our eyes, and, before we know it, fear will dominate everything else in our environment.

We can let our fear turn us against our own lives or we can allow our fear to open our eyes to great possibilities and greater results. Whatever our fear is, it is our personal key to our unknown capabilities and possibilities.

Character of Fear

Mutual Understanding

Fear expresses love too; it absorbs all energy into itself, and, before we wake up, fear has already drained all confidence from us.

Fear can turn us from good to bad, but the bad will look considerably better by the time fear has finished frightening us about everything in our lives.

Fear recognises difference as opposition, and it will make us consider difference as being the opposite.

Fear will tell us why we can't go forward, and it will show us why regression is better.

Fear will design; it can design our lives.

Fear is the best leader; it will show us every possible wrong turn but will never give us a way out.

Fear is narrow-minded; it only allows us to see what we are lacking in the midst of abundance, and it will employ greed continuously as a bounty hunter.

Fear reads consequences as punishments, and it considers results to be benefits for us.

Fear is defensive; it will always defend us if we allow it to.

Fear multiplies our goals; it takes our mind and then everything else.

Fear is an enabler; it teaches us how we should be treated.

Nothing initiates fear more than our weakened self.

To fear, anxiety is death; it influences us to shoot ourselves in the foot before aiming for the real target.

Fear sweeps things under the rug and then makes us clean the surface.

Fear keeps tabs on us and checks in sporadically to ensure we are compliant.

Fear takes opportunities for our own benefit rather than giving priority to our environment.

Fear is a control freak; it only sees itself in the multitude. Its instincts to lead and control us will kick in to protect its interests.

Fear recognises isolation as protection, and relates this to our fear as a form of strength.

Fear is the elephant in the room that we can only approach with courage.

We are all in fear; no one is greater than another.

Fear is our master; we will do whatever it asks, as long as we are safe.

Fear is a tool; it will help us to fix all that is wrong for its own benefit.

Fear is our superpower; it helps us do the unthinkable and the impossible.

Forms of Fear

Approach

Fear is one big aspect of our lives, whether we are in fear or not.

It encompasses our morals, ethics, life principles, behaviours, environment and interactions that build some trust in the community, which allows for culture and methods by which a result is achieved.

If fear is the centre of it all, then fear is life.

Nobody can live without fear, so why believe you can conquer it? For every fear conquered, there is a greater one ahead.

As frightening as fear is, it is an opportunity to be courageous. Knowing the source of our fear, and understanding its aims, objectives and time span could help us manage it accordingly.

Now that we know our fear is the "**f**easible **e**xperience of **a**nticipated **r**esults", our fear is our propellant, and where we go from here is up to us.

Acknowledgements

Thought processes, actions, reactions and outcomes have psychological effects on our experiences, and these experiences influence our beliefs, ethics and lifestyle.

These continuous influential factors shape our behaviour in communication and interaction with ourselves and our environment. This is what I have found out about myself throughout my growth process, whether logical or illogical; rational or irrational.

The most interesting part of our lives is that, even today, we all still hold significance in each others' lives and what could have a major impact and stand as a hindrance in the process of attaining our goals, can also become a powerful tool for our success.

I have progressively activated value through knowledge, understanding, wisdom and courage to handle my fears and I am getting better results because of every single person I know and have known throughout my journey.

My parents, siblings, family, friends and acquaintances from my younger years, teachers, mentors, role models, lecturers and assistants; school and university mates; work colleagues, business partners, everyday man and woman including boys and girls. You have all contributed to this journey and helped me retrace my steps, and listen to my mind and pay attention to my own emotions and reactions to see results for what they are - rather than what I think or say they should be.

You have all added values to me becoming the man I am today. Discovering and developing the process of building my own environment and coexistence, has shown me how to understand and put my fear reactions in context. I have also discovered how to reflect on our perception, and dissect our unrecognised; counter-reactions that make us who we are and what we have become.

As I have grown to pen my thoughts today, I acknowledge your influence upon my journey and I say thank you.

Bibliography

'A to Z' List of Phobias: Learn about 100+ types of phobia and enhance your word power, Hitbullseye, 2020

Anxiety and Phobia: What are specific phobias, Jessica Truschel, Remedy Health Media, February 24, 2020.

Courage: How to harness fear and be a little braver, Rebecca B.L Robinson, June 4, 2018.

Humans are born irrational, and that has made us better decision-makers. Olivia Goldhill, Quartz Media, 2020.

Meaning of fear in English, Lexico.com, 2020.

Fear, Dictionary.com, LLC, 2020.

Mythology: Definition, Joshua J. Mark, 31, October, 2018.

What is anthropophobia, and how can you manage fear of people? Jaime R. Herndon, healthline.com, April 2, 2018.

Bibliography